African History Trivia

Unveiling the Remarkable Journey from Ancient Civilizations to Modern Africa with 480 Intriguing Questions and Answers

Welcome Aboard, Check Out This Limited-Time Free Bonus!

Ahoy, reader! Welcome to the Ahoy Publications family, and thanks for snagging a copy of this book! Since you've chosen to join us on this journey, we'd like to offer you something special.

Check out the link below for a FREE e-book filled with delightful facts about American History.

But that's not all - you'll also have access to our exclusive email list with even more free e-books and insider knowledge. Well, what are ye waiting for? Click the link below to join and set sail toward exciting adventures in American History.

Access your bonus here

https://ahoypublications.com/

Or, Scan the QR code!

Table of Contents

Introduction

Are you prepared to plunge into an entire continent filled with ancient wonders, formidable empires, and transformative innovations? Get ready for an unforgettable trip through time because "African History Trivia" is your new family-friendly road-trip game.

This book, revealing the deep hues of African history, is long overdue. Whether you're a history lover or new to this amazing continent, this book covers it all. Intro to the World is filled with engaging trivia questions, fascinating facts, and captivating stories as you explore the hidden gems, groundbreaking achievements, and inspiring people who have made Africa's remarkable history – and who continue to shape its bright future.

What to Expect:

"African History Trivia" is for young explorers aged 12 to 16. It'll take you on a journey through different periods in African history, from the staggering ancient kingdoms that predated European civilization to colorful cities and sophisticated technology in contemporary Africa.

How You'll Play the Game:

- **Multiple Choice:** Consider the multiple choice questions and make an informed guess.

- **True or False:** This format will challenge you to recognize fact versus myth. Do you think you are aware of the facts regarding a historical event? Try to pinpoint the myths.

- **Fill-in-the-Blanks:** These questions ask you to remember key historical facts by completing the missing information.

- **Timeline Challenges:** In this game, you'll be testing your knowledge of historical events by putting them in the correct chronological order. Can you chart the course of Africa's incredible history?

- **'Who am I?' Sections:** These sections will provide you with clues about an African celebrity. Can you utilize your knowledge to try and guess who it is?

Every chapter covers a particular topic, drawing you further into:

- **Ancient Kingdoms:** Discover the fantastic achievements of kingdoms like Kush and Axum that flourished centuries before European civilization took hold.

- **The Mysterious Nile:** Discover the great Nile River, the lifeline of so many ancient civilizations, and find out how it influenced African life.

- **West African Empires:** Explore the mysteries of mighty empires such as Mali, Ghana, and Songhai, who controlled the gold trade for centuries.

- **Africa's Global Impact:** Did you know that Africa was at the core of building the ancient world economy? Prepare to be amazed!

- **Dynamic Cultures:** Explore the rich traditions and varied ethnic groups that render Africa a distinctive melting pot of cultures.

- **The Scramble for Africa:** This book powerfully depicts this period when European powers competed to conquer African territory and its enduring impact.

- **Independence Movements:** Honor the bravery and tenacity of Africans who struggled for their freedom, which resulted in independence throughout the continent.

- **Modern Marvels:** Get ready to be astounded by Africa's emerging cities and state-of-the-art technological innovations.

- **Voices of the Continent:** Meet influential Africans who made history and continue to inspire generations today.

Benefits Beyond Trivia:

Far more than a casual entertainment quiz book, "African History Trivia" is your key to a better understanding of Africa. You'll discover new information along with:

A New Point of View: Question your assumptions and develop a new point of view on a continent full of culture, innovation, and resilience.

Better Memory: Trivia questions sharpen your memory and allow you to recall information enjoyably.

Problem-Solving Skills: Answering challenging questions teaches you critical thinking and problem-solving skills.

A Passion for Learning: The book will instill a passion for learning more about the intriguing subject of African history.

So, take a pen, sit down with your friends, and be prepared to unlock the mysteries of Africa's incredible past. As you work through these pages, don't forget that there are no incorrect answers – only chances to discover and learn. With every question you answer and every puzzle you crack, you'll be unraveling an exciting tale of a continent that still inspires people today.

Chapter 1: Africa's Ancient Kingdoms

Prior to the time when the iconic pyramids punctuated the Egyptian heavens and great empires emerged on the rich Nile River, Africa was already a cradle of civilization, bustling with strong and advanced kingdoms. These same ancient marvels endured for centuries, leaving behind a heritage of breathtaking architecture, artistic innovations, and multi-layered societal hierarchies. How much, though, do you know of these lost giants of old? Prepare to dust off your history hat and travel back in time to go on the thrilling adventures of Africa's ancient kingdoms.

A vintage map of Africa.[1]

Multiple Choice

Prepare to test your knowledge about Africa's awe-inspiring ancient kingdoms. Returning in time, see if you can answer these multiple-choice questions about these powerful civilizations. From pyramid-building pharaohs to flourishing empires, Africa's ancient past is full of fascinating stories waiting to be discovered.

1. Which of these ancient kingdoms was known as "The Land of Gold?"
   A) Kush
   B) Axum
   C) Ghana
   D) Mali

2. The iconic pyramids of Giza were built during the reign of which pharaoh?
   A) Ramses II
   B) Tutankhamun
   C) Khufu
   D) Hatshepsut

3. Meroë, a city-state south of Egypt, was known for its production of:
   A) Gold
   B) Iron
   C) Papyrus
   D) Glass

4. The ancient city of Great Zimbabwe was the capital of which kingdom?
   A) Songhai
   B) Kanem-Bornu
   C) Kush
   D) Zimbabwe

5. The earliest known writing system in Africa was developed in:
   A) Egypt
   B) Ethiopia
   C) Mali
   D) Ghana

Fascinating Fact: Did you know that the ancient Egyptians weren't the only ones who built pyramids? The Nubian kingdom of Kush also constructed pyramids, some of which are still standing today. These pyramids, however, tend to be smaller and steeper-sided than their Egyptian counterparts.

6. Which kingdom is the Queen of Sheba, a legendary figure mentioned in the Bible, believed to have hailed from?

   A) Axum

   B) Kush

   C) Ghana

   D) Mali

7. The Nok culture, known for its impressive terracotta sculptures, flourished in what is now:

   A) Egypt

   B) Nigeria

   C) Ethiopia

   D) South Africa

Lesser-Known History: Nok culture, which existed in what is modern-day central Nigeria from 500 BCE to 200 AD, is still something of an archeological enigma. They left no written records, as the Egyptians did. Historians reconstruct their history from the hundreds of distinctive terracotta sculptures that were discovered. The life-sized and smaller-sized figures of humans and animals inform us of their beliefs, clothing, and hairstyles.

8. The ancient West African kingdom of Ghana derived its wealth from controlling which trade good?

   A) Salt

   B) Ivory

   C) Gold

   D) Textiles

9. The city of Timbuktu, a major center of learning in the Middle Ages, was part of which ancient empire?

   A) Ghana

   B) Mali

   C) Songhai

   D) Kanem-Bornu

10. Trade between ancient African kingdoms and other civilizations helped to spread which important crop?

   A) Maize (corn)

   B) Wheat

   C) Rice

   D) Cotton

True or False

Get ready to sort fact from fantasy in this "True or False" quiz. It is time to test your knowledge about Africa's ancient mighty kingdoms. Were they great pyramid builders? Did they trade a strange commodity? Read each statement carefully and determine if it is true or false.

1. The ancient Egyptians were the only civilization in Africa to build pyramids.

   o   True

   o   False

2. The kingdom of Kush, located south of Egypt, was known for its vast libraries containing scrolls on astronomy and philosophy.

   o   True

   o   False

3. The Nok culture, famous for its terracotta sculptures, thrived in what is now South Africa.

   o   True

   o   False

4. The Queen of Sheba is believed to have visited King Solomon from the ancient West African kingdom of Mali.

   o   True

   o   False

5. Hieroglyphics, a complex writing system, was developed in ancient Mesopotamia, not Africa.

   o   True

   o   False

6. The ancient city of Great Zimbabwe was built entirely out of mudbrick.
   o True
   o False

7. The kingdom of Ghana derived its wealth primarily from its trade in ivory and salt.
   o True
   o False

8. The Songhai Empire, which included the famous city of Timbuktu, was located in present-day Nigeria.
   o True
   o False

9. Trade between ancient African kingdoms and other civilizations helped to introduce cotton cultivation to Africa.
   o True
   o False

10. The Great Pyramid of Giza was built as a tomb for Pharaoh Ramses II.
    o True
    o False

Fascinating Fact: You may have known that ancient Carthage (in what is now Tunisia) was among the greatest rivals of Rome, but did you know that the Phoenicians founded Carthage some 814 years before Christ? Carthage developed into a mighty sea power, controlling maritime routes across the Mediterranean Sea. The Punic Wars, the series of wars fought between Carthage and Rome, were among the most enduring and costly of the ancient wars.

Fill in the Blank

Test your knowledge about the great civilizations of ancient Africa. Fill in the blank with the most fitting answer.

1. The Kushites, a powerful kingdom centered at Napata, were located along the Nile River in what is now modern-day _____.

2. Great Zimbabwe, known for its towering stone structures, was the capital of the _____ kingdom.

3. The city of _____, located in what is now Nigeria, was once a major center of trade and learning in West Africa.

4. The kingdom of Axum, known for its obelisks and its adoption of Christianity, was located in present-day _____.

5. The vast and prosperous kingdom of Mali, founded by Sundiata Keita, was famous for its abundant supplies of _____.

6. The impressive stone statues on Easter Island were created by the Rapa Nui people, who are believed to be descendants of people from _____.

7. The matriarchal society of _____, located in what is now Ghana, was known for its skilled metalworkers.

8. The kingdom of _____, located in present-day Senegal, was known for its cavalry and control of important trade routes.

9. The ancient city of Carthage, a major rival of Rome, was founded by the _____.

10. The pyramids of _____, located in Sudan, are some of the oldest pyramids in Africa.

Lesser-Known Story: Candace of Meroë, a title used by several Kushite queens, became a powerful symbol of resistance against Roman expansion in Africa.

Short Answers

Africa has a rich history filled with powerful kingdoms and empires that flourished across the continent. From West Africa's trade centers to the monumental pyramids of Egypt, these civilizations left behind a remarkable legacy. Test your knowledge of Africa's ancient kingdoms by answering the following short-answer questions.

1. Name one famous kingdom of West Africa and briefly describe its role in regional trade.

_____

_____

_____

_____

_____

2. What was the primary building material used for the pyramids of Giza?

_____

_____

_____

_____

3. Kush was an ancient kingdom located along the Nile River. Briefly describe its relationship with Egypt throughout history.

_____

_____

_____

_____

4. Great Zimbabwe is a fascinating archeological site in southern Africa. What is the estimated timeframe for when this city flourished?

_____

_____

_____

_____

5. Many ancient African kingdoms were skilled metalworkers. Briefly describe one object commonly crafted from metal.

_____

_____

_____

_____

_____

6. What was the approximate geographic location of the Axumite Empire?

_____

_____

_____

_____

7. The rich soil of the Nile Valley allowed for a surplus of crops. Briefly describe one crucial crop cultivated in ancient Egypt.

_____

_____

_____

_____

_____

8. Apart from pyramids, what other architectural wonder is associated with the ancient city of Meroë?

_____

_____

_____

_____

9. Oral traditions played a significant role in preserving history in many African cultures. Briefly describe one example of an oral tradition.

_____

_____

_____

_____

_____

10. Carthage was a powerful North African city-state. Who were their main rivals in the ancient Mediterranean world?

_____

_____

_____

_____

_____

Fascinating Fact: Unlike many other civilizations, Ghana did not rely on coins. Instead, they used a system based on gold dust. The purity and weight of the gold dust determined its value.

Timeline Challenge

Can you put these remarkable African civilizations in their proper historical order?

1. Place these ancient African civilizations chronologically:
    1. Kingdom of Kush
    2. Great Zimbabwe
    3. Ancient Egypt
    4. Kingdom of Ghana

_____

_____

_____

_____

_____

2. Order the following from earliest to latest:
    1. The Nok Culture
    2. The building of the Great Pyramid of Giza
    3. The rise of the Songhai Empire
    4. The flourishing of the Kingdom of Axum

_____

_____

_____

_____

3. Arrange these developments chronologically:
    1. The invention of hieroglyphics in Egypt
    2. Construction of Great Zimbabwe
    3. Meroë becomes a major center for iron production
    4. The spread of maize cultivation in Africa

    _____
    _____
    _____
    _____
    _____

4. Put these West African empires in the correct order of their prominence:
    1. Ghana Empire
    2. Mali Empire
    3. Songhai Empire

    _____
    _____
    _____
    _____
    _____

5. Sequence the following based on their reign:
    1. Pharaoh Khufu
    2. Queen Hatshepsut
    3. Ramses II

    _____
    _____
    _____
    _____
    _____

6. Order these events chronologically:
    1. The development of the Meroitic script
    2. The decline of the Kingdom of Kush
    3. The rise of the Kingdom of Axum

_____
_____
_____
_____
_____

7. Arrange these based on when they were built:
    1. The pyramids of Giza
    2. The stone structures of Great Zimbabwe
    3. The pyramids of Meroë

_____
_____
_____
_____
_____

8. Put these trade goods in the order of their rising importance in African trade routes:
    1. Gold
    2. Salt
    3. Ivory

_____
_____
_____
_____
_____

9. Sequence the following based on when they became centers of learning:
    1. The University of Timbuktu
    2. The Library of Alexandria
    3. Hieratic Writing Schools in Egypt

_____
_____
_____
_____
_____

10. Order these crops chronologically based on their introduction to Africa:
    1. Cotton
    2. Maize (corn)
    3. Wheat

_____

_____

_____

_____

_____

Answers

Multiple Choice Answers

1. **C) Ghana** (The kingdom of Ghana, flourishing between 700 and 1200 AD, was nicknamed "The Land of Gold" due to its strategic location along major trade routes and control of vast goldfields in West Africa. These gold reserves fueled Ghana's economic prosperity for centuries, allowing it to establish a powerful military and influence neighboring regions.)

2. **C) Khufu** (The reign of Pharaoh Khufu (2543-2436 BCE) is credited with the construction of the Great Pyramid of Giza, the largest of the three pyramids and one of the Seven Wonders of the Ancient World. The exact methods used to build these massive structures remain a topic of debate and fascination for archeologists and engineers today.)

3. **B) Iron** (The city-state of Meroë in the Kingdom of Kush, located in Sudan, was renowned for its advanced iron-smelting techniques. These techniques allowed the Meroites to take sturdy iron weapons, tools, and implements. Their development and use of iron was largely responsible for their success and wealth.)

4. **D) Zimbabwe** (Great Zimbabwe was the capital of the Kingdom of Zimbabwe, which flourished between the 13th and 16th centuries AD in southern Africa. This impressive city featured massive stone structures, including a hilltop enclosure, towering walls, and a complex known as the "Great Enclosure." Archeologists are still debating the exact purpose of these structures, but Great Zimbabwe stands as a testament to the architectural and engineering achievements of this ancient African kingdom.)

5. **A) Egypt** (Hieroglyphics, a complex writing system that combines pictures and symbols, emerged in ancient Egypt shortly before 3100 BCE. Hieroglyphs were used for everything from recording religious texts and royal pronouncements to everyday administrative tasks. Egyptians also developed a cursive form of hieroglyphics known as hieratic and a cursive form called demotic for faster writing.)

6. **A) Axum** (The legendary Queen of Sheba, known for her visit to King Solomon in Jerusalem, is believed by some to have originated from the kingdom of Axum, located in what is now

Ethiopia and Eritrea. Axum was a powerful trading state that flourished from around the 3rd century BCE to the 6th century AD.)

7. **B) Nigeria** (The Nok culture, named after a village where their distinctive terracotta sculptures were first discovered, thrived in central Nigeria between 500 BCE and 200 AD. These impressive works of art depict human figures with elaborate hairstyles and scarification, as well as various animals. The lack of written records from the Nok culture makes these sculptures even more valuable for understanding their society, beliefs, and artistic skills.)

8. **C) Gold** (The West African kingdom of Ghana's wealth stemmed largely from its control of the gold trade. Situated along major trade routes, Ghana levied taxes on gold mined within its territory and from neighboring regions. This steady flow of gold allowed Ghana to build a powerful military and expand its influence throughout West Africa.)

9. **B) Mali** (Timbuktu, a renowned center of learning in the Middle Ages, flourished during the reign of the Mali Empire (1226 – 1670 AD). The city boasted a famous university and attracted scholars from across the Islamic world to study subjects like mathematics, astronomy, medicine, and law. The gold trade also enriched Timbuktu, making it a major commercial and intellectual hub.)

10. **A) Maize (corn)** (Trade routes between ancient African kingdoms and other civilizations facilitated the spread of various crops. Maize, or corn, native to the Americas, is believed to have reached Africa through trade routes as early as 2000 BCE. This new crop became a dietary staple for many African societies, contributing to agricultural diversification and food security.)

True or False Answers

1. **False** (Several ancient African kingdoms, including Kush, built pyramids. While the Egyptian pyramids are the most famous, these other structures stand as a testament to the architectural achievements of various African civilizations. Notably, the pyramids of Kush tend to be smaller and steeper-sided than their Egyptian counterparts.)

2. **False** (The kingdom of Kush, a powerful state south of Egypt, was known for its production of iron and its skilled metalworkers. While they may have had some written records, there's no evidence of vast libraries containing scrolls on astronomy and

philosophy. Unlike the Egyptians, the details of Kushite writing remain undeciphered, making it difficult to reconstruct their extensive knowledge base.)

3. **False** (The Nok culture flourished in what is now central Nigeria, not South Africa. Their impressive terracotta sculptures provide valuable insights into their society and artistic expression. Dating back to around 500 BCE, the Nok culture remains somewhat of an archeological mystery. Unlike the Egyptians, they haven't left behind any written records. Historians piece together their story through the hundreds of unparalleled terracotta sculptures unearthed. These life-size and smaller-scale figures depict humans with elaborate hairstyles and scarification, as well as various animals, offering clues about their beliefs, clothing, and even hairstyles.)

4. **False** (The Queen of Sheba is believed to have originated from the kingdom of Axum, located in what is now Ethiopia and Eritrea, not Mali. The legendary Queen of Sheba, known for her visit to King Solomon in Jerusalem, has captured imaginations for centuries. While the exact details of her story remain shrouded in mystery, some historical accounts place her origin in the kingdom of Axum. This powerful trading state flourished from around the 4th century BCE to the 10th century AD.)

5. **True** (Hieroglyphics, a complex writing system combining pictures and symbols, originated in ancient Egypt.)

6. **False** (Great Zimbabwe was built using a dry stone construction technique, where large granite blocks were carefully fitted together without mortar. This method demonstrates the remarkable engineering skills of the Zimbabwe people. Great Zimbabwe was the capital of the Kingdom of Zimbabwe, which flourished between the 11th and 16th centuries AD in southern Africa. The impressive stone structures, including a hilltop enclosure, towering walls, and a complex known as the "Great Enclosure," continue to fascinate archeologists and historians today.)

7. **False** (The kingdom of Ghana's wealth stemmed largely from its control of the gold trade. Situated along major trade routes, Ghana levied taxes on gold mined within its territory and from neighboring regions. This steady flow of gold allowed Ghana to build a powerful military and expand its influence throughout West Africa.)

8. **False** (The Songhai Empire flourished in West Africa, encompassing parts of present-day Mali, Niger, and Mauritania. It was not located in Nigeria. The Songhai Empire (1430-1591 AD) rose to prominence after the decline of the Mali Empire. The city of Timbuktu, a renowned center of learning during the Middle Ages, became a major part of the Songhai Empire. The gold trade also enriched Timbuktu, making it a major commercial and intellectual hub.)

9. **False** (Cotton cultivation is believed to have originated in Asia and was introduced to Africa much later, likely through trade with Arab traders. Trade routes between ancient African kingdoms and other civilizations facilitated the spread of various crops. Maize (corn), native to the Americas, is believed to have reached Africa through trade routes as early as 2000 BCE. This new crop became a dietary staple for many African societies, contributing to agricultural diversification and food security.)

10. **False** (The Great Pyramid of Giza was built during the reign of Pharaoh Khufu, not Ramses II. Khufu's reign is estimated to be around 2589 to 2566 BCE, while Ramses II ruled much later, from 1279 to 1213 BCE. The Great Pyramid of Giza is the oldest of the three pyramids at Giza and is considered one of the Seven Wonders of the Ancient World. The exact methods used to build these massive structures remain a topic of debate and fascination for archeologists and engineers today.)

Fill-in-the-Blank Answers

1. **Sudan** (The Kushite kingdom was not merely copycats of Egyptian civilization. They adopted and adapted Egyptian religious practices, creating their unique variation. They even conquered Egypt for a time, ruling from the city of Thebes for about a century, between 760 and 656 BC. This period is known as the Kushite XXV Dynasty.)

2. **Kingdom of Zimbabwe** (The origins of the builders of Great Zimbabwe remain somewhat mysterious. While the Shona people are often associated with the city, recent research suggests there may have been multiple cultural influences at play. The impressive stone structures, built without mortar, are a testament to the engineering skill and social organization of the builders.)

3. **Kanem-Bornu** (Kanem-Bornu was a major trading center for centuries, dealing in salt, gold, and slaves. It also had a strong intellectual tradition, with scholars who wrote on a variety of subjects, including law, history, and medicine. The empire's long history saw its capital move several times, and its influence spread across a vast area.)

4. **Ethiopia** (The Axumite Empire was one of the first civilizations to adopt Christianity as its state religion. This happened in the early 4th century AD under King Ezana. The adoption of Christianity had a profound impact on Axumite art and architecture, and the country became a center for Christian scholarship.)

5. **Gold** (Mansa Musa, one of the most famous kings of Mali, is said to have given away massive quantities of gold while on a pilgrimage to Mecca in 1324. This pilgrimage is estimated to have involved a caravan of tens of thousands of people and hundreds of tons of gold. Mansa Musa's generosity helped to spread his fame and establish Mali's reputation as a wealthy kingdom.)

6. **Polynesia** (The exact reasons for the decline of the Rapa Nui civilization on Easter Island remain a subject of debate. Some theories point to environmental degradation, such as deforestation or overfishing, as a contributing factor. Others suggest that internal conflict or social collapse may have played a role. The Rapa Nui people's impressive statues, known as moai, continue to fascinate archeologists and tourists today.)

7. **Ashanti** (The Ashanti people were highly skilled in goldworking, and their craftsmen produced a wide variety of jewelry, ornaments, and other objects. They developed a unique lost-wax casting technique that allowed them to create intricate and detailed pieces. Ashanti goldwork was prized throughout West Africa and beyond.)

8. **Waalo** (The rise of the Waalo kingdom was due in part to its strategic location at the mouth of the Senegal River. The Senegal River was a vital trade route that connected West Africa with North Africa and the Mediterranean world. By controlling this river crossing, the Waalo kingdom was able to collect taxes on goods and exert influence over regional trade.)

9. **Phoenicians** (The Carthaginians were a powerful maritime people who established trade routes throughout the Mediterranean and beyond. They were skilled shipbuilders and inventors, and they are credited with developing several innovations in shipbuilding, navigation, and warfare. Their most famous conflict was the Punic Wars, a series of three long and bloody wars fought against Rome between 264 and 146 BC. Despite their impressive navy, Carthage was ultimately defeated by Rome, leading to the city's destruction.)

10. **Meroë** (The Kushite kingdom eventually shifted its center of power from Napata to Meroë, further south along the Nile. Meroë flourished for centuries, becoming a major center of iron production and trade. The city was also known for its rich artistic tradition, with elaborate jewelry, pottery, and sculptures being produced by Meroitic artisans. The kingdom of Meroë eventually declined around the 4th century AD, likely due to a combination of factors such as climate change and internal conflict.)

Short Answers

1. **Ghana:** Ghana, flourishing between 300 and 1100 AD, was a major trading kingdom in West Africa. It controlled important trade routes for gold, which was highly valued throughout the Mediterranean world, and salt, a vital necessity for both food preservation and consumption. Ghanaian merchants also traded other goods like cola nuts, slaves, and textiles. Their control over these routes and ability to tax goods passing through their territory made them incredibly wealthy and influential.

2. **Stone:** The pyramids of Giza were constructed primarily from limestone blocks, some weighing an astonishing 2.5 tons. Egyptians quarried these massive stones from nearby locations and transported them using ramps, water, and ingenuity.

3. **Kush:** The relationship between Kush and Egypt was complex and ever-changing. Sometimes, they co-existed peacefully, engaging in trade and cultural exchange. At other times, they clashed over resources and power. For example, Kush occasionally served as a tributary state to Egypt, but they also rebelled and even conquered parts of Egypt. Queen Amanishakheto of Kush (c. 1 AD) is believed to have led a successful military campaign against the Romans, even briefly conquering Egypt.

4. **Great Zimbabwe:** The city of Great Zimbabwe is estimated to have flourished between 1200 and 1500 AD. It was the capital of the Kingdom of Zimbabwe and remains one of the most captivating archeological sites in sub-Saharan Africa. The city's immense stone structures, built without mortar, are a testament to the advanced architectural skills of its inhabitants.

5. **Tools and Weapons:** Iron was a commonly used metal for crafting a variety of objects in many African kingdoms. Skilled metalworkers used iron to create tools for agriculture, such as hoes and axes, which helped them cultivate crops more efficiently. They also used iron to forge weapons like swords and spears, essential for hunting, defense, and warfare.

6. **Ethiopia and Eritrea:** The Axumite Empire was located in present-day Ethiopia and Eritrea. It thrived from roughly the 3rd century to the 6th century AD and was a major power in the region.

7. **Wheat:** The rich soil of the Nile Valley, replenished by annual floods, allowed ancient Egyptians to cultivate a surplus of crops. One of the most crucial crops was wheat. Egyptians used wheat to make bread, a staple food that fueled their large population.

8. **Temples:** Meroë, an ancient city located along the Nile in present-day Sudan, was known for its grand temples dedicated to various deities. These temples showcased the advanced architectural techniques of the Kushite people. Many of the temples were built from red brick and adorned with intricate carvings and hieroglyphs.

9. **Epic Poems:** Oral traditions played a vital role in preserving history and culture in many African societies that did not have a written language. One example of an oral tradition is the use of epic poems. Griots, or professional storytellers, would recite these long poems that recounted historical events, lineages of rulers, cultural values, and religious beliefs.

10. **Rome:** Carthage's main rivals in the Punic Wars were the Roman Republic. The Punic Wars were a series of three brutal conflicts that spanned over a century (264-146 BC) and ultimately resulted in Rome's destruction of Carthage. These wars had a profound impact on the entire Mediterranean world, shaping the course of history.

Timeline Challenge Answers

1. Ancient Egypt, Kingdom of Kush, Kingdom of Ghana, Great Zimbabwe.

2. The building of the Great Pyramid of Giza, The Nok Culture, The flourishing of the Kingdom of Axum, The rise of the Songhai Empire.

3. After the invention of hieroglyphics in Egypt, Meroë became a major center for iron production. The construction of Great Zimbabwe was followed by the spread of maize cultivation in Africa.

4. Ghana Empire, Mali Empire, Songhai Empire.

5. Pharaoh Khufu, Queen Hatshepsut, Ramses II.

6. The development of the Meroitic script, The rise of the Kingdom of Axum, d) The decline of the Kingdom of Kush.

7. The pyramids of Giza, The pyramids of Meroë, The stone structures of Great Zimbabwe.

8. Salt, Gold, Ivory.

9. Hieratic writing schools in Egypt, The Library of Alexandria, The University of Timbuktu.

10. Wheat, Maize (corn), Cotton.

Your journey through Africa's remarkable past begins with its ancient kingdoms. From the awe-inspiring pyramids of Egypt to the gold-rich empire of Ghana, these civilizations laid the groundwork for Africa's rich history. You've explored the ingenuity of Kush's iron production and the artistic mastery of the Nok culture. Trade routes fostered cultural exchange, spreading crops like maize and knowledge like hieroglyphics. This glimpse into Africa's ancient past reveals a continent brimming with innovation, power, and enduring legacies. Now, turn the page and dive deeper into Ancient Egypt's captivating story.

Chapter 2: A Journey Through Ancient Egypt

Travel back in time and get ready to be awed by the glory of Ancient Egypt. In this chapter, you will travel back to the world of pharaohs, mighty pyramids, and an otherworldly civilization. You'll decipher the codes of hieroglyphics, visit the crowded market squares, and find out the secret of the mummification technique. It's time to journey down the Nile River and appreciate marvels like the Great Sphinx and the Valley of the Kings.

Get ready to be spellbound by the tales of mighty pharaohs such as Ramses II and the amazing Cleopatra. This journey into Ancient Egypt is an unforgettable experience filled with exciting discoveries and

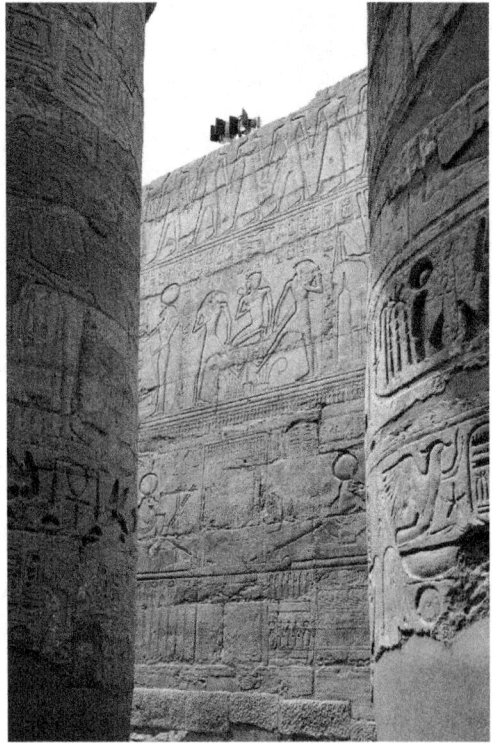

There is so much architectural history when it comes to Ancient Egypt.[2]

ageless wonders. It'll take you back in time when gods governed, pyramids touched the heavens, and the Nile River flowed smoothly along a fantastic culture.

Stunning Innovations of Ancient Egypt

The ancient Egyptians' imagination was not confined to pyramids of wonder and splendid temples. They were also innovative inventors who left behind a heritage of practical and spectacular innovations that still influence us today. Some of the standouts are:

- **Papyrus:** Well before paper in the form you're accustomed to, the Egyptians created a writing surface from the papyrus reed that grew abundantly along the Nile River. Papyrus sheets served to document everything from religious writings and administrative records to personal correspondence and literature. This was a revolutionary tool for communication and record-keeping in the ancient world.

The Ancient Egyptians used papyrus sheets to create records of everything.[3]

The Solar Calendar: Unlike most all other cultures, which were lunar in character, the Egyptians created a solar calendar, which was constructed around 3000 BCE. The Egyptians based their calendar on the coincidence of the star Sirius with the Nile's annual flood and employed a 365-day calendar with three seasons of four months each, crowned by five epagomenal days. With some modifications, this calendar became the foundation of modern calendars.

Medical Marvels: Egyptians were also skilled doctors and surgeons <u>and</u> performed advanced operations like fixing broken limbs and cataract removal. They understood anatomy and herbal remedies thoroughly, and even their surgeons used crude anesthetics for some operations. Though religiously driven, their mummification process also attests to an intimate familiarity with human anatomy and preservation.

The Ramp and the Lever: These machines assisted in hauling massive stone blocks to build huge pyramids and temples. The Egyptians utilized ramps to move giant stone blocks incrementally into position. The lever's principle was utilized in many tools to hoist heavier items and transport construction materials with more ease.

The Water Clock: Not only was calendar timekeeping practiced. The Egyptians also created the ingenious water clock, the clepsydra, to measure time by day or night. The ingenious instrument utilized the steady flow of water to measure the passing of time.

Cosmetics and Beauty Products: Personal grooming and hygiene were important to Egyptians. They created various cosmetics, including eyeliner (called *kohl*), ointments, and perfumes. These were not all for vanity; even some cosmetics offered protection from the hot sun.

These are just some of the incredible inventions and innovations that Ancient Egypt produced. Their ingenuity and persistence in seeking solutions still astound people today, a tribute to the strength of human ingenuity throughout the ages.

Famous Pharaohs and Their Legacies

Ancient Egypt has some cool stories about strong pharaohs. Let's look at a few of these rulers and what they left for us to see.

- **Tutankhamun:** King Tut is probably the most well-known pharaoh. His tomb was found almost intact in 1922. He ruled from 1333 to 1323 BCE, but his tomb shows us how wealthy pharaohs were. This find made a lot of people interested in ancient Egypt again.

  Here's a fun fact: King Tut's original name was Tutankhaten. He changed it to honor the god Amun.

King Tut.[4]

- **Cleopatra VII Philopator:** The last pharaoh of Ancient Egypt. She was a smart and tough leader. Cleopatra faced many challenges to keep her throne. She formed key partnerships with Julius Caesar and Mark Antony.

  But she was more than just a politician. Cleopatra was also good at diplomacy. She had a strong interest in art and science.

  Here's a fun fact: Cleopatra came from a long line of Macedonian Greeks who ruled Egypt after Alexander the Great. She was the first in her family to learn the Egyptian language!

Cleopatra was the last active pharaoh of Ancient Egypt.[5]

- **Ramses II:** King Ramses II, also known as Ramses the Great, ruled from 1279 to 1213 BCE. He was one of Egypt's most powerful pharaohs, reigning for an extended period. He built some incredible structures, such as the temples in Karnak and Luxor. Ramses was also a powerful military leader. He fought heavily against the Hittites.

Here's a fun fact: Ramses II had more than 200 wives and concubines, which is an interesting fact. He fathered at least one hundred children!

Statue of Ramses II.[6]

These are just a handful of the great pharaohs who altered the path of Egyptian history. Each king left their imprint, from grand temples to developments in art and science. Their legacies continue to inspire awe and provide light on the intriguing story of Ancient Egypt.

Sidebar: Festival Fun!

The ancient Egyptians enjoyed a good festival. The Nile's inundation was cause for tremendous excitement because it delivered good soil and promised a plentiful harvest. The Heb Sed celebration was a unique occasion to reaffirm the pharaoh's sovereignty and authority. Osiris' mysteries were intricate rites centered on the god's death and rebirth, which provided promise for life after death.

Multiple Choice

Unravel the mysteries of Ancient Egypt with these challenging multiple-choice questions. Put your knowledge to the test and discover some fascinating facts along the way.

1. What was the primary purpose of the Egyptian pyramids?

   A) Temples for worship

   B) Royal palaces

   C) Tombs for pharaohs

2. The Egyptians developed a complex writing system known as:

   A) Cuneiform

   B) Hieroglyphics

   C) Mayan glyphs

3. The ancient Egyptians were skilled in the art of:

   A) Mummification

   B) Metalworking

   C) Both A and B

4. The annual flooding of the Nile River was crucial for the Egyptians because the flood:

   A) Provided a source of drinking water

   B) Deposited fertile soil on the land

   C) Marked the beginning of the new year

5. The Egyptians created a calendar based on the following:

   A) The phases of the moon

   B) The movements of the stars

   C) The annual flooding of the Nile

6. What was the most common building material used in ancient Egypt?

   A) Marble

   B) Sandstone

   C) Mudbrick

7. Cleopatra, the last active pharaoh of Ancient Egypt, was descended from:
   A) Romans
   B) Greeks
   C) Persians

8. King Tutankhamun's tomb, discovered in 1922, was famous for:
   A) Its vast empty chambers
   B) The incredible amount of gold
   C) The curse of the pharaoh

9. The Egyptians believed in a complex afterlife. The process of mummification aimed to:
   A) Preserve the body for the afterlife
   B) Appease the gods
   C) Both A and B

10. The Great Sphinx of Giza is a giant statue with the head of a human and the body of a:
    A) Lion
    B) Hawk
    C) Bull

Sidebar: Cracking the Code: Hieroglyphics

Hieroglyphics are not simply drawings on ancient walls. They are rather symbols for both sounds and words. The ancients used them to document everything.

Sidebar: Building with Mudbrick

The Egyptians were incredible builders. They used mudbrick, a sun-dried mixture of mud and straw. This material was sturdy, easy to work with, and easily accessible near the Nile River.

Sidebar: The Mystery of the Missing Mummies!

Most pharaohs were lavishly buried with treasures to aid them in the afterlife. However, tomb robbers often plundered these sites throughout history. King Tut's tomb was remarkably untouched, leaving behind a treasure trove of artifacts that offered a window into ancient Egyptian life.

Image Identification

1. This massive structure is most famous for being:

Famous structure.[7]

Response: _____

    A) A palace for pharaohs

    B) A tomb for pharaohs

    C) A temple for the gods

2. This carved beetle symbolizes:

Carved beetle.[8]

Response: _____

   A) War and strength
   B) Rebirth and transformation
   C) Protection and the sun god

3. This preserved body is wrapped in linen and bandages. It is most likely:

Preserved body wrapped in linen and bandages. [9]

Response: _____

    A) A wealthy merchant

    B) A pharaoh

    C) A commoner

4. This long sheet of material was used for:

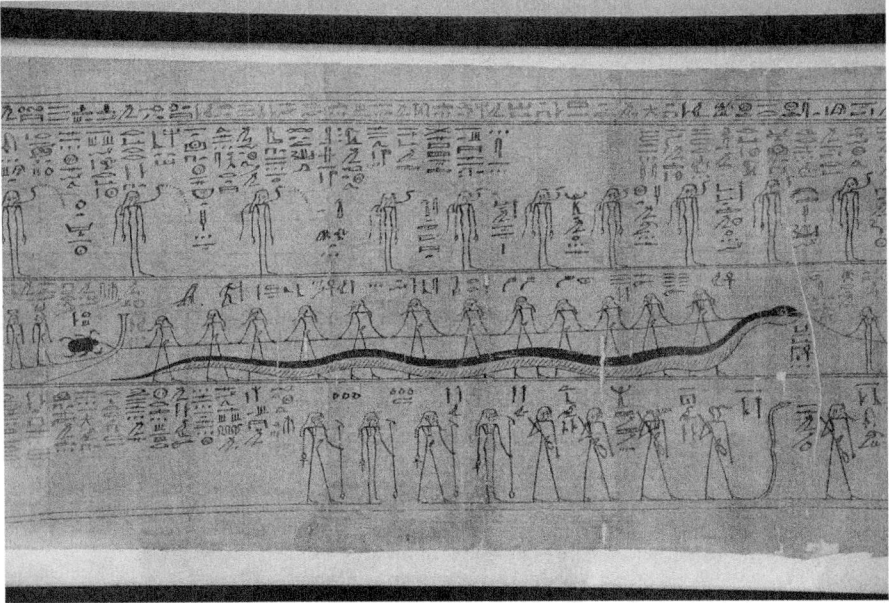

Long sheet of material.[10]

Response: _____

    A) Building walls

    B) Writing

    C) Clothing

5. This small figurine placed in a tomb was believed to:

Small figurine.[11]

Response: _____

    A) Ward off evil spirits

    B) Help the deceased with chores in the afterlife

    C) Represent a servant of the pharaoh

6. This creature has the body of a lion and the head of a human or a pharaoh. It represents:

This creature has the body of a lion and the head of a human or a pharaoh. [12]

Response: _____

    A) Strength and power

    B) Royal authority and wisdom

    C) Both A and B

7. This symbol resembles a cross with a loop on top. It represents:

This symbol represents a cross with a loop on top.[13]

Response: _____

A) Death and the afterlife

B) Life and well-being

C) The Nile River

8. This oval with a line underneath is used to enclose:

Oval with a line underneath.[14]

Response: _____

A) Hieroglyphs representing a pharaoh's name

B) Scenes of daily life

C) Religious offerings

9. The uraeus is a raised cobra on the pharaoh's headdress. It symbolizes:

What does a uraeus symbolize?[15]

Response: _____

    A) Connection to the sun god, Ra

    B) Protection from enemies

    C) Divine power and royalty

10. Identify what this hieroglyph represents:

Hieroglyph.[16]

Response: _____

A) Water

B) Sun

C) Life

Sidebar: Nile Innovation

The ancient Egyptians were ingenious inventors. They developed the shaduf, a lever system used to irrigate their fields. Papyrus, a writing surface made from reeds along the Nile, revolutionized communication. Mudbrick, a cheap and strong building material, was used to construct everything from homes to temples.

True or False

Unveil the truth behind the myths and mysteries of Ancient Egypt! Answer these true or false questions and discover fascinating facts along the way.

1. The ancient Egyptians believed in a single, all-powerful god.
   - ○ True
   - ○ False
2. Cleopatra spoke fluent Egyptian.
   - ○ True
   - ○ False
3. The Great Sphinx of Giza originally had a beard.
   - ○ True
   - ○ False
4. Papyrus, the writing material used by the Egyptians, was made from the leaves of a papyrus plant.
   - ○ True
   - ○ False
5. The ancient Egyptians were the first civilization to invent writing.
   - ○ True
   - ○ False
6. The Nile River flows from north to south.
   - ○ True
   - ○ False
7. Cats were revered and considered sacred animals in ancient Egypt.
   - ○ True
   - ○ False
8. Egyptians invented the concept of zero.
   - ○ True
   - ○ False
9. The Eye of Horus, a symbol of protection and good health, was depicted as a full eye.
   - ○ True
   - ○ False

10. Hieroglyphics are simply pictures, not a true writing system.
    o True
    o False

Sidebar: Pyramid Power

Building the pyramids was an enormous feat of engineering and human collaboration. While the exact methods used remain debated, archeological evidence suggests a skilled workforce of craftsmen, laborers, and architects likely contributed to their construction.

Short Answers

Get ready to dig deep into ancient Egypt! Answer these short-answer questions and uncover fascinating facts along the way.

1. What was the name of the writing system developed by the ancient Egyptians?

    Response: _____.

2. What natural phenomenon played a crucial role in Egyptian agriculture?

    Response: _____.

3. What was the purpose of the pyramids?

    Response: _____.

4. What was the process of preparing a body for the afterlife called?

    Response: _____.

5. Name a famous pharaoh known for his vast building projects.

    Response: _____.

6. What daily life essentials did the Egyptians invent from papyrus reeds?

    Response: _____.

7. What was the name of the sun god worshipped by the ancient Egyptians?

Response: _____.

8. The Great Sphinx of Giza has the body of a lion, but what is on its head?

Response: _____.

9. What was the capital of the Old Kingdom of Egypt?

Response: _____.

10. Describe one significant contribution of ancient Egypt to modern society.

Response: _____.

Match the Following

Test your knowledge of ancient Egypt by matching the following terms and descriptions!

1. Match these famous Egyptian pharaohs with their notable achievements.

Tutankhamun	Ruled during the New Kingdom and expanded the Egyptian empire.
Cleopatra	A famous pharaoh known for their vast building projects, including Abu Simbel.
Ramses II	The last active pharaoh of Ancient Egypt.

2. Match the following Egyptian gods and goddesses with their domains.

Rs	God of the underworld, associated with death and rebirth.
Bastet	Cat goddess, associated with protection and good health.
Osiris	Sun god – considered the king of the gods.

3. Match the following Egyptian inventions with their uses.

Papyrus	A writing surface made from papyrus reeds.
Mudbrick	A simple irrigation tool used to raise water.
Shaduf	A type of brick made from mud and straw, used for construction.

4. Match the following Egyptian structures with their descriptions.

Pyramid	A giant statue with the head of a human and the body of a lion.
Sphinx	A massive stone structure with a square base and sloping sides – was used as a tomb for pharaohs.
Obelisk	A tall, slender, four-sided monument that tapered toward the top.

5. Match the following pharaohs with their nicknames.

Khufu	The Great Builder (known for his role in constructing the Great Pyramid of Giza).
Hatshepsut	The First King (considered the founder of the first unified Egyptian state).
Menes	The Female Pharaoh (one of the few female pharaohs in Egyptian history).

6. Match the following festivals with their celebrations.

Heb Sed	A festival marking the pharaoh's jubilee and continued reign.
The inundation of the Nile	A joyous celebration marking the annual flooding of the Nile River.
Osiris's mysteries	Rituals re-enacting the death and rebirth of the god, Osiris.

7. Match the following parts of a temple complex with their functions.

Pylon	The most sacred room housing the statue of the deity.
Sanctuary	A large hall with rows of columns, used for religious ceremonies.
Hypostyle Hall	A large rectangular gateway at the entrance of the temple complex.

8. Match the following pharaohs with their pyramids.

Khufu	The Bent Pyramid (known for its unusual shape).
Sneferu	The Great Pyramid of Giza (one of the Seven Wonders of the Ancient World).
Djoser	The Step Pyramid (an early pyramid with a unique layered structure).

9. Match the following animals with their significance in ancient Egypt.

Scarab beetle	Associated with rebirth and the sun god, Ra.
Cat	Revered as a protector and a symbol of the goddess Bastet.
Crocodile	Feared predator associated with danger and power.

10. Match the following colors with their symbolism in ancient Egypt.

Gold	Represented life, growth, and rebirth.
Green	Associated with royalty, power, and the sun god, Ra.
Blue	Symbolized the sky, water, and creativity.

Sidebar: Divine Dominion

The ancient Egyptians worshipped a plethora of gods and goddesses, each with their own jurisdiction and significance. Ra, the solar deity, was regarded as the gods' ruler, responsible for creation and life. Osiris ruled the underworld and was associated with death and rebirth. Bastet, represented as a cat, was a protective deity linked with cats and females.

Answers

1. **C) Tombs for pharaohs** (The pyramids were monumental tombs designed to house the bodies of pharaohs for eternity.)

2. **B) Hieroglyphics** (Hieroglyphics were a complex writing system used in ancient Egypt for thousands of years.)

3. **C) Both A and B** (The Egyptians were skilled in mummification, a process used to preserve bodies for the afterlife. They were also masters of metalworking, creating tools, weapons, and jewelry using techniques that impressed the ancient world.)

4. **B) Deposited fertile soil on the land** (The annual flooding of the Nile brought rich silt deposits that were perfect for growing crops. This predictable flood cycle was the foundation of Egyptian agriculture.)

5. **A) The phases of the moon** (The Egyptian solar calendar was based on the cycles of the moon, consisting of 365 days with additional feast days.)

6. **C) Mudbrick** (Mudbrick was the most common building material in ancient Egypt. It was cheap, readily available, and strong enough for many structures.)

7. **B) Greeks** (Cleopatra belonged to the Ptolemaic dynasty, founded by a Macedonian Greek general after Alexander the Great's conquest of Egypt.)

8. **B) The incredible amount of gold** (King Tut's tomb contained a vast array of treasures, including gold jewelry, furniture, and even solid gold funerary masks. This discovery offered unprecedented insights into the opulence of the pharaohs.)

9. **C) Both A and B** (Mummification aimed to preserve the deceased's body for the afterlife journey and appease the gods, ensuring a successful transition.)

10. **A) Lion** (The Great Sphinx of Giza is a majestic statue with the head of a human and the body of a lion. It remains one of the most recognizable symbols of ancient Egypt.)

Image Identification Answers

1. **B) A tomb for pharaohs** (Pyramids were primarily built as tombs for pharaohs to house their bodies in the afterlife.)

2. **B) Rebirth and transformation** (The scarab beetle pushes a ball of dung, similar to the sun pushing a ball of light across the sky. It was seen as a symbol of rebirth and the cycle of life.)

3. **B) A pharaoh** (Mummification was a complex and expensive process, usually reserved for pharaohs and the wealthy elite.)

4. **B) Writing** (Papyrus was made from the papyrus plant and used for writing important documents, religious texts, and stories.)

5. **B) Help the deceased with chores in the afterlife** (Shabti dolls were believed to come alive in the afterlife and perform tasks for the deceased.)

6. **C) Both A and B** (Sphinxes combined the strength of a lion with the intelligence of a human, representing both royal authority and wisdom.)

7. **B) Life and well-being** (The Ankh is one of the most recognizable symbols of Ancient Egypt and represents life, breath, and well-being.)

8. **A) Hieroglyphs representing a pharaoh's name** (Cartouches were used to enclose the names of pharaohs and important figures, protecting them and ensuring their legacy.)

9. **C) Divine power and royalty** (The uraeus, a raised cobra, was associated with the goddess Wadjet, protector of pharaohs. It symbolized divine power and protection.)

10. **A) Water** (The wavy lines depicted water in ancient Egyptian hieroglyphs.)

True or False

1. **False** (The ancient Egyptians believed in a complex pantheon of gods and goddesses, each with their domain and significance.)

2. **True** (Cleopatra, the last active pharaoh of Ancient Egypt, was remarkably well-educated. While Greek was the language of administration during her reign, Cleopatra was one of the few Ptolemaic rulers to learn the ancient Egyptian language! This fluency helped her connect with her Egyptian subjects and solidified her position as pharaoh.)

3. **True** (Archeological evidence suggests the Great Sphinx originally had a beard, which has since eroded.)

4. **True** (Papyrus was a game-changer in the history of communication. Egyptians developed a clever way to transform the papyrus reed, abundant along the Nile River, into thin sheets for writing. These sheets were then joined together to create scrolls upon which they recorded everything from religious texts to shopping lists.)

5. **True** (The ancient Egyptians developed hieroglyphics, one of the earliest forms of writing.)

6. **False** (The Nile River flows from south to north.)

7. **True** (Cats held a special place in ancient Egyptian society. They were seen as protectors against vermin and associated with the goddess. Bastet. Egyptians often kept cats as pets and even mummified them after death to accompany them in the afterlife.)

8. **False** (The concept of zero originated by Mayans and Indians, not ancient Egyptians.)

9. **False** (The Eye of Horus is one of the most recognizable symbols in ancient Egyptian art. It represents protection, royal power, and good health. Interestingly, the Eye of Horus is not a full eye. It is depicted with a stylized falcon head and an eyebrow missing a portion of the eye.)

10. **False** (Hieroglyphics are a complex writing system that combines pictures representing sounds and words.)

Short Answers

1. **Hieroglyphics**

2. **The flooding of the Nile River** (The ancient Egyptians thrived, thanks to the predictable flooding of the Nile River. Each year, the river overflowed its banks, depositing fertile silt that nourished the land and allowed for abundant crops. This annual flood cycle was the lifeblood of Egyptian agriculture.)

3. **Tombs for pharaohs.**

4. **Mummification** (Mummification was a complex and time-consuming process that Egyptians believed was necessary to preserve the body for the afterlife. The organs were removed and placed in canopic jars, and the body was dried with salts and wrapped in linen bandages. The entire process could take up to 70

days!)

5. **Ramses II** (possible answers could include other famous pharaohs like Khufu or Hatshepsut.)

6. **Writing material (papyrus)** (Papyrus was an ingenious invention of the ancient Egyptians! They transformed the papyrus reed, abundant along the Nile, into thin sheets for writing. These sheets were then joined together to create scrolls upon which they recorded everything from religious texts to medical knowledge.)

7. **Ra.**

8. **A human.**

9. **Memphis** (Memphis was a powerful city during the Old Kingdom of Egypt. Located at a strategic point along the Nile River, it served as a center of government, trade, and religion. The city remained an important center of Egyptian culture for thousands of years.)

10. **Answers can vary but could include:** The development of a calendar system, advancements in medicine, the concept of a centralized government, or the invention of papyrus as a writing material.

Match the Following

1. Tutankhamun/Ruled during the New Kingdom and expanded the Egyptian Empire; Cleopatra/The last active pharaoh of Ancient Egypt; Ramses II/Famous pharaoh known for his vast building projects, including Abu Simbel.

2. Ra/Sun god – considered the king of the gods; Bastet/Cat goddess, associated with protection and good health; Osiris/God of the underworld, associated with death and rebirth.

3. Papyrus/A writing surface made from papyrus reeds; Mudbrick/A type of brick made from mud and straw, used for construction; Shaduf/A simple irrigation tool used to raise water.

4. Pyramid/A massive stone structure with a square base and sloping sides – used as a tomb for pharaohs; Sphinx/A giant statue with the head of a human and the body of a lion; Obelisk/A tall, slender, four-sided monument that tapered toward the top.

5. Khufu/The Great Builder (known for his role in constructing the Great Pyramid of Giza); Hatshepsut/The Female Pharaoh (one of the few female pharaohs in Egyptian history); Menes/The First King (considered the founder of the first unified Egyptian state.)

6. Heb Sed/A festival marking the pharaoh's jubilee and continued reign; The inundation of the Nile/A joyous celebration marking the annual flooding of the Nile River; Osiris's mysteries/Rituals reenacting the death and rebirth of the god, Osiris.

7. Pylon/A large rectangular gateway at the entrance of the temple complex; Sanctuary/The most sacred room, housing the statue of the deity; Hypostyle Hall/A large hall with rows of columns, used for religious ceremonies.

8. Khufu/The Great Pyramid of Giza (one of the Seven Wonders of the Ancient World); Sneferu/The Bent Pyramid (known for its unusual shape); Djoser/ The Step Pyramid (an early pyramid with a unique layered structure.)

9. Scarab beetle/Associated with rebirth and the sun god, Ra. (Scarabs roll dung into balls, similar to the way the Egyptians believed the sun god, Ra, rolled the sun across the sky); Cat/Revered as a protector and a symbol of the goddess, Bastet; Crocodile/Feared predator associated with danger and power.

10. Gold/Associated with royalty, power, and the sun god, Ra; Green/Represented life, growth, and rebirth; Blue/Symbolized the sky, water, and creativity.

The legacy of Ancient Egypt continues to influence art, literature, and architecture around the world. You can still learn from their innovations in agriculture, medicine, and astronomy.

In this chapter, you've explored the wonders of this fascinating civilization, from the life-giving Nile River to the towering pyramids. You've learned about the powerful pharaohs, the complex system of gods and goddesses, and the daily lives of the people.

Ancient Egypt continues to capture people's imaginations today. Its architectural marvels are a testament to its engineering skills, its hieroglyphics slowly reveal its stories, and its mummies offer a glimpse into its beliefs about the afterlife.

Chapter 3: The Great Empires of West Africa

Forget about the Pharaohs for a moment. Let's talk about Mansas. West Africa has a very intriguing past. It had strong empires that lasted a long time. Ghana, Mali, and Songhai prospered in a variety of environments.

In this chapter, we shall travel back in time. You will meet leaders such as Mansa Musa. He was known as a pleasant and successful leader. His actions had a considerable influence.

Prepare to discover incredible structures, inventive ideas, and bustling trade routes. You'll see how gold helped their economy and elevated their profile around the world.

Great African Empires

Although ancient Egypt is commonly seen as the main African civilization in historical talk, the continent is full of empires and kingdoms that flourished before, during, and after the reign of Egypt. So, let's get to the workings of some of these great civilizations and let us understand their unique contributions to our society.

The Mali Empire (1226 - 1670 AD)

Mali was known as the "Land of Gold" because it controlled important gold-producing areas in West Africa. Under the reign of the renowned Mansa Musa, it reached its highest peak in the 14th century. His extraordinary pilgrimage to Mecca made him even more famous, as he was said to have given away massive amounts of gold along the way, gaining fame as a wealthy and devout ruler. The empire was also distinguished by many thriving trade networks, with such cities as Timbuktu emerging as centers of knowledge and commerce.

Unique Aspects:

- **Center of Knowledge:** The city had been the home of the famed Sankore University, attracting scholars from every corner of the Islamic world.

- **Stunning Architecture:** Under the reign of Mansa Musa, the capital was modified, complete with the Djinguereber Mosque.

- **Gold Trading Powerhouse:** Mali had its gold mines and trade routes, which made it one of the major sources of wealth and influence.

Kush Kingdom (1069 BC-350 AD)

Resting on the Nile River, south of Egypt, the Kingdom of Kush was a power throughout its long history, starting as a trading partner and rival to Egypt until it occupied and ruled Lower Egypt for a while. Though Kushite rulers took on certain Egyptian prerogatives; they continued cultivating their own culture, with the god Amun being in a predominant position.

Unique Aspects:

- **Nile River Knowledge:** The people of Kush developed advanced systems of irrigation and agriculture to work the fertile plains along the Nile.

- **Pyramids Builders:** The Kushite kings, like the Egyptians, built pyramids for their royal envelopes, but these would be each steeper and pointier.

- **Fusion of Cultures:** Kush was influenced by Egypt but maintained its traditions, and produced its unique styles of art and beliefs.

Great Zimbabwe (1100-1450 AD)

Situated in southern Africa, Great Zimbabwe was still a civilization full of enigmas. This kingdom took its name from its great capital city and boasted some of the unpopular stone constructions – built without mortar. The purpose of these is up for debate, with theories suggesting they were royal enclosures, religious centers, or storehouses.

Unique Features:

- **Stone Construction:** The tall towers of granite at Great Zimbabwe bore testimony to the development of architectural skill in the society.

- **Trade Network:** Great Zimbabwe was a partner in regional trade in which golden bits, ivory, and other exotic items were exchanged for value.

- **Mystery Remains:** The reasons for the decline of Great Zimbabwe remain obscure, intensifying its magic for archeologists and historians alike.

These empires represent merely a minor fraction of Africa's rich history beyond Egypt. From the great riches of Mali to the architectural wonders of Great Zimbabwe, these civilizations placed their mark on African history.

African Innovations & Discoveries

Beyond the political and economic might of the empires of Africa, there stretched an ocean of innovation and discovery. From sophisticated urban planning to technological and scientific advancement, Africa contributed significantly to progress, much of which has filtered into today's world. Some examples of those stellar achievements are:

Pioneering Architects and Urban Planners

- **Benin (1200-1897):** Now located in Nigeria, Benin was famous for its splendid capital, Benin City. The city was endowed with large roads, moats, and walls, highlighting the grandeur behind the architectural and planning prowess of the kingdom. Archaeological evidence demonstrates that the urban environment had a highly organized setup with separate quarters for craftworkers, royal residences, and shrines.

- **Great Zimbabwe (1100-1450):** Once again, the stone works in series in Great Zimbabwe told of the great genius concerning architecture and engineering. The layout of the city with enclaves, towers, and passageways shows pronounced marks of planning and organization.

Centers of Learning and Knowledge Production

- **The Universities of Timbuktu (989-1960 AD):** There is much more, for it is the same appeal that strikes one as the one, although with bloody trade. If one were to list the illustrious universities of Sankore in India for decades and in perpetuity, those of Timbuktu welcomed scholars from all parts of the world. That is where one found great libraries housing manuscripts on all conceivable topics, including mathematics, astronomy, medicine, and law.

- **The Ethiopian Manuscript Tradition:** For centuries, Ethiopia has been a place of great scholarship. Monks copied and preserved manuscripts on diverse topics: religious texts, historical accounts, and scientific treatises. It is from these manuscripts that one might glean an idea of life in history, culture, and scholarship in Ethiopia.

Advancements in Science and Technology

- **Iron Age in Africa:** Iron Age technology arrived in Africa centuries before it was discovered in Europe. It was, therefore, in 500 BC that the societies were attaining smelting technology with iron. With enhanced iron tools and weapons becoming available, agriculture, warfare, and daily life experienced revolutions. The applicability of black sandy soil to construction and other purposes depends on the conditions among several others that have since changed.

- **Astronomy and Calendar Systems: Agricultural Innovations**

  Several African cultures achieved significant advancements in the field of astronomy. For instance, the Dogon people of Mali possessed an extraordinarily intricate understanding of constellations and demonstrated an ability to predict complex celestial events with remarkable accuracy. Additionally, the Kingdom of Meroë, which emerged as a successor state to Kush, developed an elaborate system for tracking lunar and stellar movements, establishing a sophisticated observational calendar.

- **Crop Domestication:** Africa is considered a cradle of several important crops like sorghum, millets, and yams. The domestication of crops facilitated the growth of human populations within the continent.

- **Irrigation Techniques:** African civilizations built different types of irrigation systems to enable farming in arid and semi-arid zones. Different methods made it possible for agriculture to thrive and for complex societies to rise, in conjunction with some unique irrigation systems above the Nile River in the Kingdom of Kush.

These few examples illustrate just a fraction of the great inventions and discoveries African civilizations could boast of. From revolutionary architecture to scientific and agricultural advances, the African-rich intellectual heritage continues to challenge and enlighten people even today.

Multiple Choice

Test your understanding of the great West African empires with these multiple-choice questions.

1. Which African empire was ruled by Mansa Musa, one of the richest people in history?

   A) Mali Empire

   B) Songhai Empire

   C) Kingdom of Aksum

2. The city of Timbuktu, a renowned center of learning and trade, flourished under the rule of which empire?

   A) Ghana Empire

   B) Mali Empire

   C) Songhai Empire

3. Great Zimbabwe, known for its impressive stone structures, was located in what part of Africa?

   A) West Africa

   B) East Africa

   C) Southern Africa

4. The Kingdom of Kush, located along the Nile River, was a rival and trading partner of which ancient civilization?

   A) Persia

   B) Greece

   C) Egypt

5. The Sankore University, a prestigious center of scholarship, was located in which West African city?

   A) Djenné

   B) Gao

   C) Timbuktu

6. What was a major source of wealth for the Mali Empire?

   A) Salt

   B) Gold

   C) Ivory

7. The ingenious use of iron tools and weapons transformed African societies during which historical period?

   A) The Bronze Age

   B) The Iron Age

   C) The Neolithic Age

8. What is the name of the famous mosque built by Mansa Musa in the Malian capital?

   A) Great Mosque of Mecca

   B) Djinguereber Mosque

   C) Mosque of Ibn Tulun

9. What crop is considered to be native to Africa and played a vital role in supporting its population growth?

   A) Wheat

   B) Sorghum

   C) Rice

10. The Kingdom of Benin was known for its well-planned capital city featuring a network of avenues and moats. What is the present-day location of this kingdom?

    A) Mali

    B) Niger

    C) Nigeria

Map Pointing

Test your geography skills by identifying the locations of these major West African empires and kingdoms on the provided map!

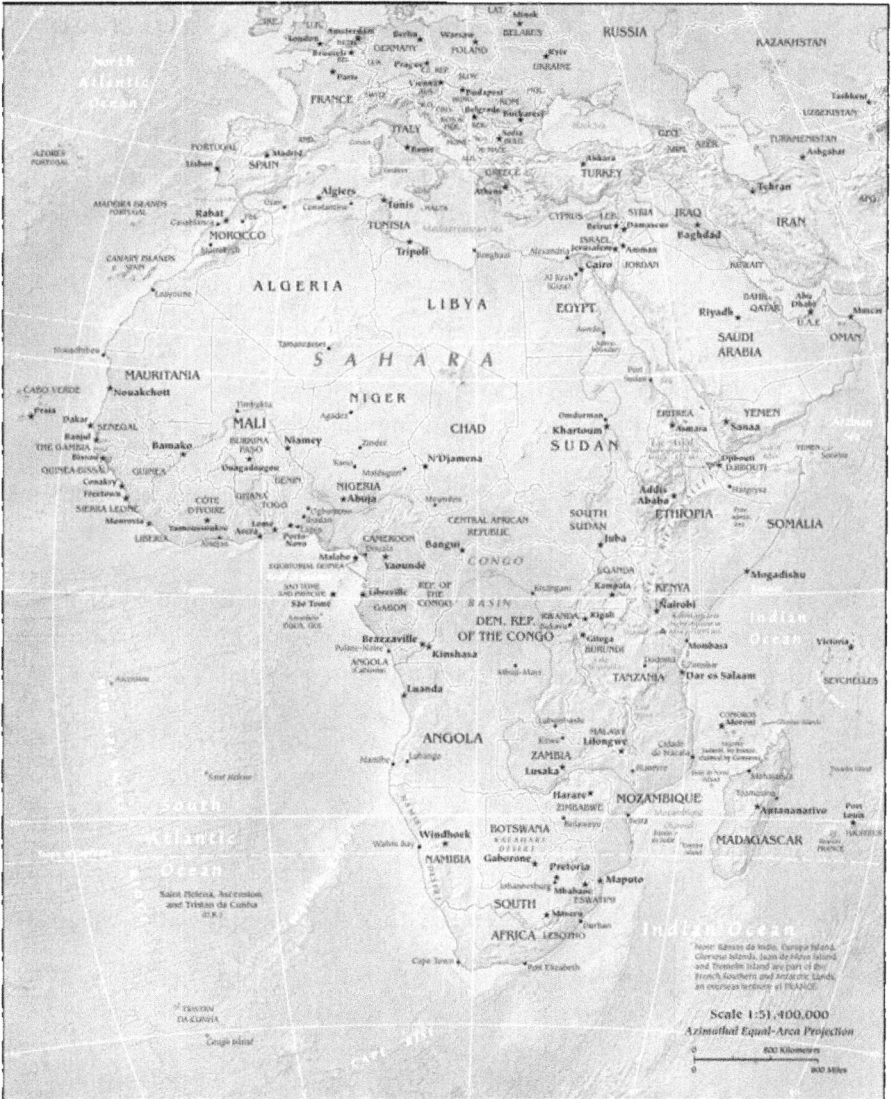

Map of Africa.[17]

1. Identify the location of the Kingdom of Ghana, which flourished as a major trading center in West Africa.

2. Pinpoint the location of the Mali Empire, which reached its peak under the illustrious leadership of Mansa Musa.

3. Locate the Songhai Empire, which rose to power after the decline of the Mali Empire.

4. Identify the approximate location of Great Zimbabwe, a southern African kingdom known for its impressive stone structures.

5. Show where the Kingdom of Kush was situated along the Nile River.

6. Can you identify the location of the city of Timbuktu, a renowned center of learning and trade during the Mali Empire?

7. Where do you think the major gold-producing regions that fueled West African empires might have been situated?

8. Based on the map, can you infer any trade routes that these empires might have utilized? For example, look for connections between gold-producing regions and major cities or empires.

9. Considering the location of the Kingdom of Kush, what other civilizations might they have interacted with along the Nile River?

10. Imagine you are a trader living in West Africa during this era. Using the map, plan a potential trade route you might take, considering factors like resource availability and geographic features.

True or False

Can you separate fact from fiction? Answer true or false for each of the following statements about the West African empires.

1. Timbuktu was an ancient center of learning and trade in Africa.
    o   True
    o   False

2. The Kingdom of Ghana was the wealthiest empire to ever exist in Africa.
    o   True
    o   False

3. Great Zimbabwe is famous for the intricate rock paintings that its inhabitants left behind.
    o   True
    o   False

4. Mansa Musa, ruler of the Mali Empire, was known for his extravagant spending habits.
    o   True
    o   False

5. The Songhai Empire absorbed the territory of the declining Mali Empire at its peak.
    o   True
    o   False

6. The use of iron tools and weapons had minimal impact on African societies.
    o   True
    o   False

7. The Kingdom of Kush adopted some aspects of Egyptian culture despite being a rival.
    o   True
    o   False

8. The universities in Timbuktu were open only to scholars from wealthy families.
    o   True
    o   False

9. Sorghum, a grain crop, is native to Europe and was introduced to Africa through trade.
   o True
   o False

10. The Great Mosque of Djenné, a landmark structure, is located in present-day Ghana.
    o True
    o False

Fill in the Blank

Test your memory and understanding of the West African empires by filling in the blanks with the appropriate term or terms.

1. The _____ civilization, known for its large stone structures, was located in present-day Zimbabwe.

2. The city of ____-_____, a renowned center of learning and trade, flourished under the rule of the Mali Empire.

3. Mansa ____-_____, the most famous ruler of the Mali Empire, was famed for his wealth and his pilgrimage to Mecca.

4. The Kingdom of ____-_____, located along the Nile River, was ancient Egypt's rival and trading partner.

5. The universities of _____ were prestigious centers of scholarship that attracted scholars from across the Islamic world.

6. What was a major source of wealth for the Mali Empire? Response:_____.

7. What historical period saw the widespread use of iron tools and weapons in Africa, transforming societies? Response:_____.

8. The Great Mosque of Djenné, a landmark structure, is located in present-day _____.

9. Sorghum is a grain crop native to Africa that plays a vital role in supporting population growth. What is another name for the region where sorghum is particularly cultivated? Response:_____.

10. The Kingdom of Benin, known for its well-planned capital city, is located in present-day _____.

West Africa's rich history extends far beyond the empires you've explored in this chapter. However, these powerful kingdoms are a testament to the ingenuity, resilience, and cultural vibrancy of the region. The empires may have risen and fallen, but their legacy continues to inspire people today.

West Africa's past is not merely a collection of dates and names. As you explore African history, you'll discover even more remarkable stories and civilizations waiting to be unearthed. Their advancements in architecture, agriculture, and ironworking technologies had a lasting impact on the continent. Their emphasis on trade and scholarship fostered connections across vast distances and laid the foundation for future generations.

Answers

Multiple Choice

1. **A) Mali Empire** (Mansa Musa was the most famous ruler of the Mali Empire.)

2. **B) Mali Empire** (Timbuktu reached its peak as a center of learning and trade during the Mali Empire.)

3. **C) Southern Africa** (Great Zimbabwe was a kingdom located in southern Africa, encompassing parts of present-day Zimbabwe, Mozambique, and South Africa.)

4. **C) Egypt** (The Kingdom of Kush, located south of Egypt along the Nile, interacted with Egypt as a trading partner and rival for some time.)

5. **C) Timbuktu** (Sankore University was a renowned center of learning situated in the West African city of Timbuktu.)

6. **B) Gold** (The Mali Empire controlled major gold-producing regions, making gold a significant source of their wealth.)

7. **B) The Iron Age** (The widespread use of iron smelting technology in Africa occurred during the Iron Age, transforming various aspects of life.)

8. **B) Djinguereber Mosque** (Mansa Musa commissioned the construction of the Djinguereber Mosque, a landmark structure in Mali.)

9. **B) Sorghum** (Sorghum is a grain crop native to Africa that plays a crucial role in supporting the growth of human populations across the continent.)

10. **C) Nigeria** (The Kingdom of Benin was located in present-day Nigeria, known for its sophisticated urban planning and impressive capital city.)

Map Pointing

1. Look for an empire in West Africa in Arabic, located roughly between modern-day Mauritania and Mali.

2. The Mali Empire should be situated west of the Songhai Empire and encompass parts of modern-day Mali, Senegal, and Guinea.

3. The Songhai Empire should be positioned east of the Mali Empire, encompassing parts of modern-day Mali, Niger, and Chad.

4. Look for the southernmost empire on the map, likely situated in present-day Zimbabwe.

5. The Kingdom of Kush should be south of Egypt, likely encompassing parts of modern-day Sudan and South Sudan.

6. Timbuktu should be within the borders of the Mali Empire, likely near the Niger River bend.

7. These regions would likely be concentrated in the westernmost part of the map, encompassing parts of modern-day Mauritania, Senegal, and Mali.

8. Trade routes likely followed the Niger River, a vital waterway that facilitated the movement of goods between different regions. One trade route connected the gold-producing regions in western Africa (present-day Mauritania, Senegal, and Mali) to the city of Timbuktu, a major trading center within the Mali Empire. Another route stretched from the gold-producing regions southward toward Great Zimbabwe, another major empire.

9. The Kingdom of Kush might have interacted with Egypt, located further north along the Nile River.

10. Here's a possible trade route you could take as a trader in West Africa:

   o Start your journey in **Djenné**, a major trading center located in the Mali Empire (modern-day Mali). Djenné was known for its production of salt, an essential commodity.

   o Travel north toward the gold-producing regions in **Wangara** (present-day southwestern Mali and southeastern Mauritania). Here, you could acquire gold, which was highly valuable for trade.

   o From Wangara, you have a few options depending on your destination and the goods you wish to trade.

   o Head west toward the city of **Timbuktu**. Timbuktu was a major center of learning and trade, where you could sell your gold for other goods like luxury items, books, or spices brought by traders from across North Africa and the Middle East.

   o Travel south toward the savanna regions. Here, you could trade your gold for items like ivory, kola nuts, or animal hides, which were produced in these regions.

- o If you're feeling adventurous, you could undertake a long journey south across the Sahara Desert to **Great Zimbabwe**. This route would be challenging due to the harsh desert environment, but the potential profits from trading gold for luxury goods from East Africa could be significant.

True or False

1. **True** (Timbuktu was a flourishing center of learning and trade during the golden age of West African empires, particularly under the Mali Empire. The city housed prestigious universities and boasted vast libraries containing manuscripts on a wide range of subjects, making Timbuktu a hub of intellectual exchange.)

2. **False** (While the Ghana Empire was a major power due to its control of the gold trade route and the accumulation of significant wealth, other empires like Mali likely surpassed its peak wealth. Mansa Musa's reign in Mali, for example, was marked by an abundance of gold, and his extravagant spending habits further solidified this perception.)

3. **False** (Great Zimbabwe is renowned for its impressive stone structures, some towering as high as 30 meters. These structures were built without mortar, showcasing the advanced architectural skills of the civilization. While rock paintings are found throughout Africa, they are not a defining characteristic of Great Zimbabwe.)

4. **True** (Mansa Musa's lavish spending habits were legendary. His pilgrimage to Mecca was a spectacle, with him reportedly bringing along a massive caravan loaded with gold. He handed out so much gold during his pilgrimage that it is said to have caused inflation in the region for a decade.)

5. **True** (The Songhai Empire, under the leadership of rulers like Sunni Ali and Askia the Great, capitalized on the decline of the Mali Empire and managed to absorb significant portions of its territory. This expansion propelled Songhai to become a major power in West Africa.)

6. **False** (The widespread use of iron tools and weapons during the Iron Age, roughly between 500 BC and 1000 AD, had a profound impact on African societies. It revolutionized agriculture, allowing for more efficient land clearing and cultivation. Iron weapons also transformed warfare, giving societies with iron technology a significant advantage.)

7. **True** (The Kingdom of Kush, located along the Nile River, south of Egypt, interacted with Egypt as a trading partner and rival for some time. Despite their rivalry, the Kushite people adopted some aspects of Egyptian culture, particularly regarding their gods. For example, they worshipped the god, Amun, though they depicted him differently than the Egyptians.)

8. **False** (The universities in Timbuktu, like Sankore, were renowned for their openness to scholars from various backgrounds. These institutions fostered a rich intellectual environment. Knowledge was seen as valuable, and these universities aimed to educate and inspire scholars regardless of their social status or wealth.)

9. **False** (Sorghum is a grain crop native to Africa, particularly the Sahel region and East Africa. Its domestication played a crucial role in supporting the growth of human populations across the continent. Sorghum is drought-resistant and thrives in hot climates, making it a valuable food source for many African societies.)

10. **False** (The Great Mosque of Djenné, a UNESCO World Heritage Site, is a landmark structure located in Mali. Built primarily of mudbrick, it is an architectural marvel known for its distinctive pyramidal towers. While Ghana also boasts rich historical sites, the Great Mosque of Djenné is not located within its present-day borders.)

Fill in the Blank

1. **Great Zimbabwe** (This kingdom, flourishing between the 11th and 15th centuries AD, was renowned for its impressive stone structures, some towering as high as 30 meters. These structures were built without mortar, showcasing the advanced architectural skills of the civilization. Great Zimbabwe is located in southern Africa, encompassing parts of present-day Zimbabwe, Mozambique, and South Africa.)

2. **Timbuktu** (This West African city became a major center of learning and trade during the Mali Empire, particularly under Mansa Musa's reign. The city housed prestigious universities like Sankore, attracting scholars from across the Islamic world. Timbuktu is located in present-day Mali.)

3. **Mansa Musa** (Mansa Musa's reign (1312-1337 AD) is considered the golden age of the Mali Empire. His leadership and focus on trade expansion led to immense wealth for the empire. Mansa

Musa's extravagant spending habits were legendary. His pilgrimage to Mecca was a spectacle, with him reportedly bringing along a massive caravan loaded with gold. He handed out so much gold during his pilgrimage that it is said to have caused inflation in the region for a decade.)

4. **Kush** (The Kingdom of Kush, located along the Nile River, south of Egypt, interacted with the Egyptians for centuries. Initially serving as a trading partner, Kush eventually rose to power and even conquered and ruled Lower Egypt for a period. Despite their rivalry, the Kushite people adopted some aspects of Egyptian culture, particularly regarding their gods. For example, they worshipped the god, Amun, though they depicted him differently than the Egyptians. The Kushite kingdom flourished from roughly 1069 BC to 350 AD.)

5. **Timbuktu** (The universities of Timbuktu were renowned for their openness to scholars from various backgrounds, fostering a rich intellectual environment. The flourishing universities of Timbuktu contributed significantly to West Africa's intellectual legacy.)

6. **Gold** (The Mali Empire controlled major gold-producing regions in West Africa, making gold a significant source of their wealth. This gold trade fueled the empire's economy and propelled it onto the world stage.)

7. **The Iron Age** (The widespread use of iron tools and weapons in Africa, roughly between 500 BC and 1000 AD, is termed the Iron Age. This period saw a significant transformation in African societies. Iron tools allowed for more efficient land clearing and cultivation, leading to increased agricultural productivity. Iron weapons also transformed warfare, giving societies with iron technology a significant advantage.)

8. **Mali** (The Great Mosque of Djenné, a UNESCO World Heritage Site, is located in Mali. Built primarily of mudbrick, it is an architectural marvel known for its distinctive pyramidal towers. The Great Mosque is not only a landmark but also a place of worship and a testament to the artistic traditions of the region.)

9. **Sahel** (Sorghum is a grain crop native to Africa, particularly the Sahel region and East Africa. Its domestication played a crucial role in supporting the growth of human populations across the continent. Sorghum is drought-resistant and thrives in hot climates,

making it a valuable food source for many African societies. The Sahel is a semi-arid region stretching across the south of the Sahara Desert.)

10. **Nigeria** (The Kingdom of Benin, known for its well-planned capital city featuring a network of avenues and moats, was located in present-day Nigeria. This kingdom flourished between the 15th and 16th centuries and was renowned for its skilled craftspeople, particularly metalworkers and artists.)

Chapter 4: Africa's Role in the Ancient World Economy

For too long, a story about Africa and its role in the ancient economic landscape has revolved around one commodity: gold. No doubt, this abundant resource acted as the lifeblood of empires and trading routes. However, Africa's many contributions to the international economy extend far beyond a reflective gloss.

The chapter harnesses the sentiments of trade and commerce across Africa. Understand how Africa made itself into an international trade center, how it became a source of diverse quality goods, and how it wielded considerable influence in shaping the economies of the old world. Prepare to drown in the sheer breadth of wares-from salt and ivory, textiles, and craftsmen's wares for such interlinked markets of the past.

Trade and Commerce in Ancient Africa

Long before, the illustrious trade routes across Africa bore life's breath before grand empires could take shape. Trading routes extended from the parching sands of the Sahara to the tropical forests of Central Africa. Supplying economic exchange and cultural interaction was this vast network of trade routes. With time, trade changed the African societies.

- **The Trans-Saharan Trade:** It was one of those great iconic routes that crisscrossed the vast Sahara Desert as an important artery of commerce for centuries. Camels - *often called the ships of the desert* - became the chief means of transporting goods such as gold, salt, and ivory-Crossing the North of the Sahara to Mediterranean markets. In turn, luxurious goods such as glass beads, textiles, and manufactured items came back for these items across the Sahara.

- **The Nile River Route:** It provided a natural channel for trade to flow both within Africa and across its continua. Grain, papyrus, and gold moved from Egypt to the southern areas as ebony and ivory moved from Central Africa to the Mediterranean. Thus the Nile facilitated the rise of such powerful kingdoms as Kush, which regimentally controlled trade along the river.

- **East African Coastline:** The trade winds of the Indian Ocean established a flourishing maritime network along the East African borders. Ships from Arabia, India, and China sailed to ports such as Mombasa and Zanzibar, where goods manufactured in various countries, spices, and ceramics were exchanged for African products like gold, ivory, and timber.

The Flow of Goods:

- **Gold:** The shimmering appeal of African gold is indubitable. This metal, which provided energy for empires, from the enormous goldfields in West Africa to Nubian mines, spurred international economies. Gold was, indeed, much more than a form of currency; it was a status symbol sought after by rulers and traders alike throughout the ancient world.

- **Salt:** Commonly referred to as the "white gold," it constituted one more critical item of such commerce. And because it is a vital food preservative and, also seasoning, the salt-producing areas in the Sahara Desert, such as the Taghaza salt mines, attracted traders from as far as Morocco.

- **Ivory:** The shining tusks of elephants were in great demand because of their beauty and multiplicity of uses. For jewelry making, decoration, or furniture, ivory was a luxury item that moved from the central African savannas to markets across the Mediterranean and beyond.

- **Other Valuable Goods:** An interesting assortment of other commodities was traded across Africa. Among those was, unfortunately, the slave trade, which applied especially to the East African coast. In addition, crops like sorghum and millet, beautiful handwoven textiles, and crafts were also Base contributions to the ancient world economic system.

The Impact of Trade:

Trade networks owe their prosperity to the following effects they brought to bear on African societies:

- **Rise of Great Kingdoms:** Exchanges across trade routes supplied states with wealth and power. Control over routes intended for visits to resources including gold mines, allowed Ghana, Mali, and Axum kingdom to gain immense power and wealth.

- **Cultural Exchange:** Besides goods, conversations on ideas and cultures took place. Trade routes became very important avenues for the dissemination of artistic styles, religious ideas, and technological advances across a variety of geographical landscapes.

- **Urbanization:** The great development of trade led to the birth of thriving urban centers. Cities served as markets where production took place as centers of administration, amplifying profitable activities.

- **Social Change:** Trade brought new social classes and opportunities to societies. Merchants became rich and financially powerful, and skilled artisans found a wider market for their wares; they even participated in trade. However, the changes were also with social inequalities in societies.

Bumping up the somewhat more market-oriented trade and commerce that early Africa touted was a driving factor behind the social changes, cultural exchanges, and great kingdoms. Africa's involvement in the ancient world economy extended beyond gaudy trinkets of gold, bequeathing a legacy that makes the continent's timescapes that much more lively and textured.

A Day in the Life of an Ancient African Society

It's adopting a perspective of history: we travel not to one location on the African continent but across an entire landscape filled with diverse cultures and lifestyles. Ranging from the commercial life in West Africa to the very high culture of the Nile Valley civilization in Egypt, nothing could compare to the living experience of the ancient Africa of those times. Here we glance at life's picture from the perspective of common people of the time belonging to various ancient African societies.

Food:

- **West Africa:** Much of the diet was made up of millet, sorghum, and yams. Such foods could be eaten paired together with stews of vegetables, lentils, and occasional meat. Sweetness came from fruits such as mangoes and palm nuts.

- **Nile Valley:** The diet consisted of cereals such as wheat, barley, and lentils, supplemented with onions and chickpeas, and were often complemented with Nile fish. Dates and figs were sweetening fruits to Egyptians.

- **East Africa:** Sorghum and millet remained staple grains; bananas and plantains were also parts of the diet. Some herding societies, such as the Maasai, gathered milk, blood, and meat from their cattle.

Clothes:

- **Across Africa:** Clothing styles were varied in direct relation to the climate and the availability of materials in such a region. In the hotter regions, people may wear simple wraps made of woven plant fibers or animal skins. In the cooler parts, people may work wearing a tunic or wool or cotton-draped garment. In various areas, ornamentation made with beads, shells, or metal attracted popular attention.

Housing:

- **West Africa:** Houses were generally built of mudbrick or wood, with thatched roofs. A number of extended families might have spent a compound together, each family having its own cooking, sleeping, and storing house.

- **Nile Valley:** They built their homes from mud brick, with flat roofs, whereby they sat on the roofs at leisure or used them for drying crops. The rich lived in comfortably walled and painted houses.

- **East Africa:** Here, housing styles were multiple. Some lived in circular huts of mud and dung; others built houses on stilts in swampy areas.

Education:

- **Formal education:** Formal schooling was mainly for elite people or boys destined to become priests. However, all children were taught what was needed in society by their families. Boys would learn skills in hunting, herding, or handcraft, while girls would be schooled in cooking, weaving, and nursing.

- **Storytelling:** Storytelling represents an important aspect of education and entertainment. Folktales and myths that were passed down through many generations pass on cultural knowledge, moral lessons, and historical records.

Leisure Activities:

- **Games:** Mancala, which involved deep holes and stones on a board, was one of the board games common in many cultures across Africa. Down in the South, some cultures enjoyed throwing sticks or wrestling.

- **Music and Dance:** Music and dance were an integral aspect of every social gathering and celebration. People beat the drums, played flutes, violins, and – with a really fast beat – danced lively rounds.

- **Festivals:** Festivals were filled with celebrations that gave loose to feasts, music, dancing, and storytelling as a welcomed way of giving thanks for a good harvest, marking a victory, or celebrating some other religious occasion.

Interesting Tidbits:

- **Mancala Tournaments:** Mancala tournaments were organized occasionally, with money and bragging rights on the line.

- **Wrestlers' Training:** In some cultures, strong wrestlers are still created by building themselves up with heavy stones.

- **Earliest Ancestral Worship:** Many African societies believed in ancestor worship. Thus, rituals and offerings for the dead in order to keep a spirit alive were common practices.

You begin to appreciate the diverse yet rich cultural types that had their origin in the different ancient African societies from studying their day-to-day lives. Those societies tell of their diets, lives, and many other variables that comprise their high-spirited existence.

Multiple Choice

Test your understanding of Africa's contributions to the ancient world economy with these multiple-choice questions.

1. What was a major commodity traded from West Africa along the Trans-Saharan trade routes?

   A) Spices

   B) Gold

   C) Silk

2. The Nile River provided a natural highway for trade within Africa and beyond. What product was most likely exported south from Egypt?

   A) Gold

   B) Salt

   C) Papyrus

3. The East African coastline benefited from trade winds that propelled ships from various regions. What was a common good imported to East Africa from these trade partners?

   A) Ivory

   B) Glass Beads

   C) Wheat

4. Besides gold, what other valuable resource was extracted from the Sahara Desert and highly sought after in trade?

   A) Diamonds

   B) Salt

   C) Silver

5. The development of powerful kingdoms in Africa was often linked to their control of strategic trade routes or resources. Which empire flourished in West Africa due to its proximity to major goldfields?

   A) Kush

   B) Ghana

   C) Axum

6. Trade routes not only facilitated the movement of goods but also ideas and cultural practices. What is an example of something that might have spread along trade routes in Africa?

   A) New farming techniques

   B) Artistic styles

   C) Religious beliefs

   D) All of the above

7. The growth of trade fostered the development of thriving urban centers in Ancient Africa. What is one of the primary functions these cities serve?

   A) Administrative centers

   B) Marketplaces

   C) Centers of production

   D) All of the above

8. Unfortunately, the ancient world economy also involved the slave trade. Along which African coast were slaves a significant export?

   A) West African coast

   B) North African coast

   C) East African coast

9. Unlike some societies that relied on formal schooling, many African societies emphasized learning practical skills within families and communities. What skill might a young boy learn from his father in an agricultural society?

   A) Metalworking

   B) Herding

   C) Writing

10. Storytelling played a crucial role in education and entertainment across Africa. What is one of the purposes folktales and myths served in these societies?

    A) Preserved cultural knowledge

    B) Entertained audiences

    C) Passed down historical accounts

    D) All of the above

Picture Quiz

Test your knowledge of African trade and daily life by examining these historical artifacts.

1. Identify this artifact and its use in ancient African societies.

Identify this artifact.[18]

Response: _____.

2. What was the likely function of this object in daily life?

Identify the function of this option in daily life.[19]

Response: _____.

3. What is the purpose of a mask like this in some African societies?

Identify the purpose of a map like this.[20]

Response: _____.

4. This object was likely used for what purpose in ancient African societies?

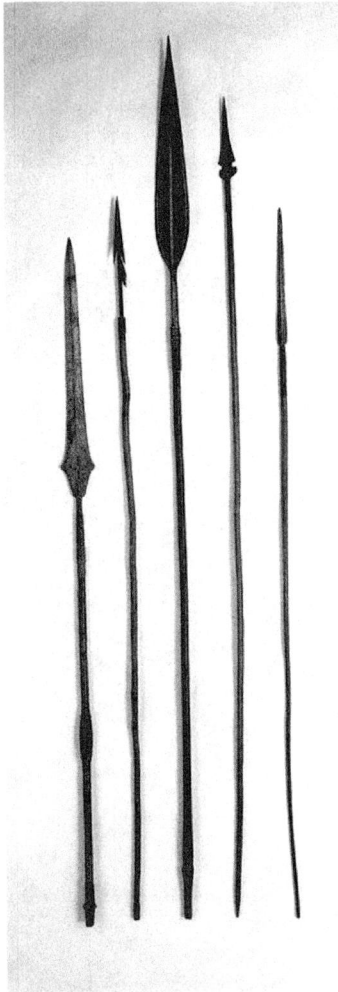

Identify the use of this artifact. [21]

Response: _____.

5. What role did this object likely play in the ancient African economy?

Identify the role this object played.[22]

Response: _____.

6. What product might have been made from this raw material?

Identify the goods made from this raw material. [23]

Response: _____.

7. What was the likely function of this object in food preparation?

Identify the function of this object for food preparation.[24]

Response: _____.

8. What can this statue tell us about the society that created it?

What does the status tell us about the society that created it?[25]

Response: _____.

9. The use of iron tools like this one likely had a significant impact on what aspect of life in ancient Africa?

Identify what aspect of life this tool had an impact on.[26]

Response: _____.

10. What role did music likely play in ancient African societies?

Identify the role music played in Ancient African societies.[27]

Response: _____.

True or False

Distinguish fact from fiction by evaluating these statements about Africa's role in the ancient world economy.

1. The Kingdom of Axum was primarily known for its trade in ivory and precious stones.
   o True
   o False

2. Salt was a valuable commodity traded across Africa because it was scarce and difficult to obtain.
   o True
   o False

3. The Nile River was not a significant factor in promoting trade within ancient Africa.
   o True
   o False

4. Only elites in African societies had access to education and learning.
   o True
   o False

5. The growth of trade routes in Africa had no impact on the development of cities.
   o True
   o False

6. Mancala, a strategic board game, was a popular pastime enjoyed by people of all ages in many African societies.
   o True
   o False

7. The Trans-Saharan trade routes relied solely on horses for the transportation of goods across the desert.
   o True
   o False

8. Gold was the only valuable resource that Africa offered to the ancient world economy.
   o True
   o False

9. The spread of Islam along trade routes did not influence some African societies.
   o True
   o False

10. All cultures within ancient Africa had the same approach to clothing and housing due to similar climates.
    o True
    o False

Fill in the Blank

Solidify your understanding of Africa's contributions to the ancient world economy by completing these fill-in-the-blank questions.

1. _____ was an important center of Islamic learning and culture in medieval West Africa.

2. The network of trade routes that crisscrossed the Sahara Desert for centuries is known as the _____.

3. Along the East African coast, ships from various regions were propelled by _____, which helped facilitate trade.

4. _____ was a valuable commodity extracted from the Sahara Desert and essential for food preservation.

5. Besides gold, another highly-prized product obtained from Africa's savannas was _____.

6. Mancala, a popular strategic board game played across Africa, involves using pits and _____.

7. The growth of trade led to the development of thriving _____ in Africa.

8. Unfortunately, the ancient world economy also involved the slave trade, with a significant export market emerging along the _____ coast of Africa.

9. In some African societies, children learned valuable skills from their families, such as _____ in agricultural communities.

10. Storytelling played a crucial role in African societies, with folktales and myths serving to preserve _____ and entertain audiences.

Answers

Multiple Choice Answers

1. **B) Gold** (West Africa was renowned for its vast gold deposits, and gold was a major commodity traded along the Trans-Saharan routes.)

2. **C) Papyrus** (Papyrus, a versatile plant used for writing material, was a significant export from Egypt.)

3. **B) Glass Beads** (East Africa imported various goods, including luxury items like glass beads, from trade partners like Arabia and India.)

4. **B) Salt** (Salt, a vital food preservative, was another highly sought-after commodity extracted from the Sahara Desert.)

5. **B) Ghana** (The Ghana Empire's proximity to major goldfields in West Africa contributed significantly to its wealth and power.)

6. **D) All of the above** (Trade routes facilitated the exchange of ideas, artistic styles, religious beliefs, and new farming techniques across vast distances.)

7. **D) All of the above** (These urban centers served as administrative hubs, bustling marketplaces, and centers for production, driving economic activity.)

8. **C) East African coast** (The East African coast witnessed a significant slave trade, with people being exported to various regions.)

9. **B) Herding** (In agricultural societies, young boys might have learned valuable skills like herding from their fathers to contribute to the family's livelihood.)

10. **D) All of the above** (Folktales and myths served the purpose of preserving cultural knowledge, entertaining audiences, and passing down historical accounts from generation to generation.)

Picture Quiz Answers

1. This is a **bead necklace**. Beads made from glass, stone, and other materials were a popular form of adornment across Africa. More than being merely decorative, they signified wealth, status, or religious beliefs.

2. This is a decorated **clay pot**. Clay pots were essential for storing food, transporting water, and even cooking. The geometric patterns might have served decorative purposes or held symbolic meaning.

3. This is a carved wooden **mask**. Masks were used in various ceremonies and rituals across Africa. They could represent spirits, ancestors, or mythical figures. The mask's intricate carvings might provide clues about its purpose in a particular ceremony.

4. This is a metal **spear**. Spears were multipurpose tools used for hunting, warfare, and defense. The long blade suggests it might have been particularly effective for hunting large animals.

5. This is a gold bar. Africa, particularly West Africa, was renowned for its gold deposits. Gold was a valuable commodity used in trade, as a form of currency, and to display wealth and power.

6. This is a coil of woven **raffia fiber**. Raffia fibers, extracted from palm trees, were widely used in Africa to make various items, such as baskets, mats, hats, and clothing.

7. This is a grinding stone. Grinding stones were used to grind grains, nuts, and seeds into flour or paste, forming the base for many African dishes.

8. This is a wooden statue depicting a seated figure. Statues like this can provide valuable insights into a society's artistic style, religious beliefs, or even depictions of important figures. The pose and clothing of the figure might offer clues about its significance.

9. This is an iron hoe. The widespread adoption of iron tools during the Iron Age (roughly between 500 BC and 1000 AD) revolutionized agriculture in Africa. Iron tools were more durable and efficient than stone tools, allowing for increased agricultural productivity and supporting larger populations.

10. This is a traditional African musical instrument. Music played a vital role in social gatherings, religious ceremonies, and celebrations across Africa. It served purposes like entertainment, storytelling, and even communication.

True or False Answers

1. **True** (The Kingdom of Axum, located in modern-day Ethiopia and Eritrea, was strategically positioned near elephant populations and sources of precious stones, making it a major center for trade in these items.)

2. **False** (While salt was valuable, it was not necessarily scarce in all regions of Africa. However, its importance for food preservation made it a highly sought-after commodity, especially in areas where it was not readily available.)

3. **False** (The Nile River served as a vital waterway for trade within Africa, facilitating the movement of goods like grain, papyrus, and gold between different regions.)

4. **False** (While formal education systems might have been limited, all children learned valuable skills from their families and communities, ensuring the transmission of knowledge and traditions.)

5. **False** (The growth of trade routes led to the development of thriving urban centers that served as marketplaces, administrative hubs, and centers of production. These cities became centers of economic activity.)

6. **True** (Mancala was a widely enjoyed game across Africa, transcending age groups and offering entertainment and strategic challenges.)

7. **False** (Camels were the primary mode of transport across the harsh Sahara due to their endurance and ability to survive for long periods without water. Horses, while used for transportation in some regions of Africa, were not well-suited for the desert environment.)

8. **False** (Africa offered a diverse range of resources to the ancient world economy, including gold, salt, ivory, crops like sorghum and millet, handcrafted textiles, and skilled artisanship.)

9. **False** (The spread of Islam along trade routes introduced new religious beliefs and practices that influenced some African societies. The level of influence varied depending on the region and existing cultural practices.)

10. **False** (While there might have been some similarities due to shared climates in certain regions, African cultures were diverse. Clothing and housing styles adapted to. local environments and cultural preferences. For example, people in hot regions might have worn light clothing made from plant fibers, while those in cooler areas might have worn heavier garments made from wool.)

Fill-in-the-Blank Answers

1. **Timbuktu** (Timbuktu was a renowned center of Islamic learning and culture in West Africa during the medieval period.)
2. **The Trans-Saharan Trade Route** (This network of trade routes connected North Africa to West Africa and facilitated the exchange of goods for centuries.)
3. **Trade winds** (Trade winds blowing along the East African coast helped propel ships from Arabia, India, and even China, fostering maritime trade.)
4. **Salt** (Salt was a vital commodity for food preservation and was extracted from various locations in the Sahara Desert.)
5. **Ivory** (Ivory, obtained from elephants, was a highly-prized luxury good used for crafting jewelry, decorative items, and furniture.)
6. **Stones** (Mancala is played with pits dug into the ground or a board with indentations, and players use small stones or other markers.)
7. **Urban centers** (These centers served as marketplaces, administrative hubs, and centers of production fueled by the growth of trade.)
8. **East African** (The East African coast witnessed a significant slave trade, with people being exported to various regions.)
9. **Herding** (In agricultural societies, young boys might learn valuable skills like herding livestock from their fathers.)
10. **Cultural knowledge** (Storytelling preserves cultural knowledge and traditions, passing them down from generation to generation.)

Africa's contributions to the ancient world economy extended far beyond a single glittering commodity. The continent offered a diverse range of resources, from salt and ivory to skilled artisanship, shaping economies and influencing cultures across the globe.

The stories of ancient Africa are not merely tales of the past. They hold profound meaning for the present. The trade networks established centuries ago continue to echo in modern-day commerce. The emphasis on craftsmanship and skilled labor resonates in the vibrant artistic traditions that continue to thrive across Africa.

Chapter 5: Ethnic Groups and Traditions Across Africa

Africa is richly diverse. From the snow-clad heights of Mount Kilimanjaro to the farthest stretches of the Sahara Desert, the landscapes are as different as their people. This chapter is going to take you on a journey, probably an interesting one, to have an interaction with some of the amazing ethnic groups that live in Africa.

You'll experience music and dance festivals, age-old traditions that have survived years, and systems of beliefs that are integrated into the daily livelihood of the people. Each ethnic group, with its own language, customs, and artistic expressions, weaves a beautiful thread into the rich cultural tapestry of Africa.

Get ready to be excited by the resilience, creativeness, and resourcefulness found in these various communities. You are about to witness how they have adapted to their environments, embraced sustainable practices, and celebrated their identities through the generations. So come on in and appreciate Africa in all its glory!

The Influence of African Art and Music

The artistic and musical traditions of Africa are as diverse and colorful as her very own people. From the exquisitely detailed sculpture of the Nok culture to the vibrant rhythms of the djembe drum, African artistic forms have enchanted audiences with power for centuries and continue to influence your world.

Modes of Artistic Expression:

- **Sculpture:** Across the continent, sculptures have been crafted from wood, bronze, terracotta, and ivory. Most of these tend to depict deities, ancestors, or mythical figures and have contributed to both religious beliefs and social values. The Nok culture's terracotta heads depicting tranquil expressions testify to the skill and ancient history of African sculpture alongside the life-sized bronze figures of the great Benin Kingdom.

- **Masquerades:** Masquerades provide an impressive alternative artistic expression existing in various African traditions. During ceremonies, rituals, and celebrations, participants wear intricately carved and flamboyantly decorated masks with feathers, beads, and fabrics. Such masks symbolize spirits, ancestors, or mythic figures that transition humans between the earthly and spiritual worlds.

- **Textiles:** The production of textiles is an age-old art form over all of Africa. The colorful woven cloths of the Kuba people from Central Africa and the exquisite indigo-dyed fabrics of West Africa illustrate a cultural identity, social status, and artistic skill. Mudcloth dyeing, strip weaving, and beadwork blend in harmoniously to enrich the tradition of African textiles.

- **Rock Art:** A rich bouquet of prehistoric rock art emerges from the Sahara Desert, where formerly a lush savanna flourished. These paintings and engravings – of animals, human figures, and hunting scenery – consciously reflect life and belief systems in those early societies of Africa.

Music:

Music in Africa is all life, weaving diverse layers of rhythms with catchy melodies and storytelling through song. Here are a few examples of this lively musical tradition:

- **Djembe:** This goblet-shaped drum, with a deeply resonant sound, is, in fact, a solid foundation for West African music. Normally played in ensembles, djembe drums produce rhythms that are full of life and vigor, thus enlivening celebrations and ceremonies.

- **Kora:** This harp-like instrument with a distinct sound is common in West Africa among the Mandinka people. The Kora accompanies storytelling through songs and has solo and ensemble forms of music, including leading epic tales.

- **Mbira:** The finger piano, made up of metal tines fixed to a wooden board, originated in South and East Africa. From a series of live thin gold-wire tines sounding plucked sounds within the nice resonance, mesmerizing codes melted into the ceremonial as well as the recreational use of its in-use today.

Global Impact:

African art and music have had a worldwide impact:

- **Visual Arts:** The aesthetic of Africa, in vivid colors and marked with geometric patterns, animated the works of countless artists, most famously Pablo Picasso and Georges Braque.

- **Music:** The rhythms of African music may be heard in jazz, blues, and salsa. African patterns of drumming and call-and-response techniques have become an integral part of these globally recognized musical styles.

- **Performance:** Dances native to Africa continue influencing modern dance standards through energy and interpretative elements and charm the world audience daily.

The influence of African art and music extends beyond aesthetics. These creative expressions base themselves on the essence, chronicle, and belief systems established by Africa's diverse communities. While involving you in bookmarks of African art and music, you will understand its legacy and, indeed, a source of endless creativity propelling artists and musicians across the globe.

Famous African Leaders and Heroes

From centuries past, African leaders and heroes have been playing their special roles in the history of their nations and shaping them into what they became, being the architects of their ambitions. Men since ancient times set the pace in courage and wisdom in leadership to inspire subsequent generations. Meet some of these personalities:

- **Hatshepsut (Egypt, 15th Century BCE):** Defying male expectations, Hatshepsut was a powerful female pharaoh in ancient Egypt who reigned in peace and prosperity for more than two decades. Under her command, expeditions occurred regarding trade and external projects, such as the magnificent mortuary temple at Deir el-Bahri, and the arts flourished.

- **Mansa Musa (Mali Empire, 14th Century CE):** Mansa Musa led the West African Mali Empire with leadership and piety. His wealth and Islamic devotion made him most famous for traveling to Mecca and leading an extravagantly grand caravan to proclaim Mali's prestige. While Mansa Musa forested, he invested in big-time infrastructure projects by commissioning mosques and promoting Islamic scholarship, giving rise to what became known as the golden age of the empire.

- **Queen Nzinga (Angola, 17th Century CE):** Queen Nzinga, a warrior queen of Ndongo and Matamba kingdoms in Angola, led a fierce resistance against Portuguese colonialism for decades. A gifted diplomat and military strategist, she constantly employed guerilla tactics and used alliances to defend her people's freedom. Nzinga remains the symbol of resistance against all oppressive forces.

- **Shaka Zulu (Zulu Kingdom, 19th Century CE):** Shaka Zulu was a visionary 19th-century leader for the kingdom of Zulu in South Africa who developed the Zulu Kingdom by way of new military warfare. Shaka connected various tribes and turned them into one of the most formidable armies. It is not surprising that some call him a prophet while others view his mass hysteria as barbarity while in some hypnotizable trance in the back of the car.

- **Nelson Mandela (South Africa, 20th Century CE):** Nelson Mandela became an international symbol of the struggle against apartheid, the most brutal and intransigent system of racial discrimination in South Africa. He didn't flee after 27 years of imprisonment because of a moral mistake directed at him; rather, he pursued a revelation that hated neither violence nor violence. Because he participated in the dismantling of this regressive party, he became President of South Africa in a historic election in 1994. A living legacy of peace, resilience, and forgiveness, recast as acts of forgiveness and peace processes, casts an enormous shadow way up to the present as humanity seeks to address the unfolding global quest for justice.

- **Maathai Wangari (20th-21st Century-Kenya):** Wangari Maathai was an environmentalist and, therefore, wielded much environmental power. She became the first black woman to be a Nobel Peace Prize Laureate; to support the Green Belt Movement, she started using tree planting as a tool for combating deforestation, poverty, and women's inequity; as an area of research, this work did not confine itself to merely environmental issues, and this research opened up ways for humans to determine their own destinies.

These are just a few of the millions upon millions who are brave, visionary, extraordinary Africans who contributed to the history of Africa's past and present.

Multiple Choice

Explore your understanding of Africa's diverse ethnic groups and traditions with these multiple-choice questions!

1. Which instrument is commonly associated with West African music?

   A) Djembe

   B) Violin

   C) Piano

   D) Tabla

2. The colorful woven cloths produced by the Kuba people of Central Africa are known as what?

   A) Kente cloth

   B) Kuba cloth

   C) Batik

   D) Mudcloth

3. Rock art depicting animals and human figures can be found in what region of Africa, once a lush savanna?

   A) East Africa

   B) West Africa

   C) The Sahara Desert

   D) Southern Africa

4. Masquerades, featuring elaborately carved masks, are a significant art form used in ceremonies and rituals across many African societies. What purpose might a masquerade serve?

A) Decoration only

B) To represent spirits, ancestors, or mythical figures

C) To frighten away evil spirits

D) All of the above

5. The intricate indigo-dyed fabrics produced in West Africa are a testament to the artistic expression and skills associated with what craft?

A) Wood carving

B) Metalworking

C) Textile production

D) Basket weaving

6. Mansa Musa, a revered leader of the West African Mali Empire, is known for his pilgrimage to Mecca and his contributions to what aspect of the empire?

A) Military expansion

B) Artistic achievements

C) Infrastructure development and scholarship

D) Trade relations with Europe

7. Queen Nzinga of Angola fiercely resisted Portuguese colonialism for decades. What strategy did she employ to defend her people?

A) Open warfare with large armies

B) Guerilla tactics and alliances

C) Diplomacy and negotiation only

D) Seeking aid from other European powers

8. Nelson Mandela, a global icon of the anti-apartheid movement in South Africa, became the country's first black president. What principle did Mandela advocate for during his presidency?

A) Violence and revolution

B) Reconciliation and forgiveness

C) Strict racial segregation

D) Military rule

9. Wangari Maathai, a Kenyan environmental activist, founded the Green Belt Movement, focusing on which two crucial issues?

A) Education and healthcare

B) Environmental conservation and women's empowerment

C) Technological advancement and economic development

D) Political reform and social justice

10. The Nok culture, known for its terracotta head sculptures, flourished in what region of ancient Africa?

A) Egypt

B) West Africa

C) East Africa

D) Central Africa

True or False

Distinguish fact from fiction by evaluating these statements about Africa's diverse ethnic groups and traditions!

1. The ancient Zimbabweans were renowned for their stone architecture.
   o True
   o False

2. All ethnic groups in Africa have the same traditional religion and belief systems.
   o True
   o False

3. Griots, or storytellers, play a vital role in preserving history and cultural traditions in many African societies.
   o True
   o False

4. The kola nut is a fruit enjoyed primarily for its delicious taste.
   o True
   o False

5. The Kente cloth is traditionally associated with the Maasai people of East Africa.
   o True
   o False

6. The intricate beadwork created by the Maasai people is primarily used for decoration.
   o True
   o False
7. Sundiata Keita, the founder of the Mali Empire, was a skilled military leader who united various Mande groups.
   o True
   o False
8. Traditional dance forms in Africa often tell stories and are not merely for entertainment.
   o True
   o False
9. The traditional coming-of-age ceremonies in many African societies mark a person's transition into adulthood.
   o True
   o False
10. The concept of Ubuntu, emphasizing interconnectedness and humanity, is a core value in many African societies.
    o True
    o False

Fill in the Blank

Solidify your understanding of Africa's diverse cultures and traditions by completing these fill-in-the-blank questions:

1. The vast continent of Africa is home to over 3,000 distinct _____, the largest number of any continent.

2. These ethnic groups are often identified by their shared _____, language, religion, and social customs.

3. The largest ethnic group in Africa is the _____, concentrated primarily in central and southern Africa.

4. The Great Rift Valley, a massive geographical trench, is a significant feature that has both _____ and _____ impacts on the distribution of ethnic groups across Africa.

5. Animism, the belief in spirits inhabiting natural objects, is a traditional religion practiced by many ethnic groups, particularly in _____ Africa.

6. Storytelling is an essential part of keeping traditions alive across Africa. These stories are often passed down through generations by _____.

7. The Griots of West Africa are known as hereditary _____, skilled storytellers, musicians, and genealogists.

8. Traditional African art forms encompass a wide variety of mediums, including sculpture, _____, and masks, which are often used in religious ceremonies and rituals.

9. _____ is known as the 'father of modern Egypt' and is credited with implementing significant reforms in the 19th century.

10. Despite its vast diversity, Africa is a continent united by a shared history, cultural practices, and a strong sense of _____.

One-Word Answer Questions

Africa is a continent rich in history and cultural diversity. From the ancient empires of the Sahel to the well-developed societies of southern Africa, each region boasts unique ethnic groups with their traditions, languages, and art forms. Test your knowledge of Africa's diverse cultures with these one-word answer questions.

1. Name the ancient African kingdom famous for its terracotta sculptures.

   Response: _____.

2. What is the traditional one-stringed fiddle from West Africa called?

   Response: _____.

3. What is the largest ethnic group in Nigeria?

   Response: _____.

4. What language is spoken by the majority of the population in Ethiopia?

   Response: _____.

5. What religion is practiced by the Dogon people of Mali?

   Response: _____.

6. What is the annual migration of millions of wildebeest in East Africa called?

   Response: _____.

7. What is the colorful woven fabric worn throughout West Africa called?

   Response: _____.

8. What South African art form features dynamic beadwork and storytelling?

   Response: _____.

9. What is the traditional coming-of-age ceremony for Maasai youth called?

   Response: _____.

10. What is the world's oldest desert located in Namibia called?

    Response: _____.

Quick Fact Match

Match the following leaders and empires/kingdoms to showcase your understanding of African history!

1. Match the leader (Shaka Zulu, Cleopatra, Haile Selassie) with their empire or kingdom.
   o Shaka Zulu ( ) Mali Empire
   o Cleopatra ( ) Zulu Kingdom
   o Haile Selassie ( ) Ancient Egypt

2. Match the ethnic group (Kuba, Maasai, Ashanti) with the traditional clothes they are known for.
   o Kuba ( ) Kente cloth
   o Maasai ( ) Shuka
   o Ashanti ( ) Kuba cloth

3. Match the art form (rock art, sculpture, mask) with the material it might be crafted from.
   o Rock art ( ) Wood
   o Sculpture ( ) Terracotta
   o Mask ( ) Paintings

4. Match the instrument (djembe, kora, mbira) with its region of origin.
   o Djembe ( ) West Africa
   o Kora ( ) Central Africa
   o Mbira ( ) East Africa

5. Match the ceremony (coming-of-age, pilgrimage, harvest) with its purpose.
   o Coming-of-age ( ) Celebrating a bountiful harvest
   o Pilgrimage ( ) Transition into adulthood
   o Harvest ( ) Journey to a sacred place

6. Match the saying (Ubuntu, Harambee, Asante sana) with its language of origin.
   - Ubuntu ( ) Swahili
   - Harambee ( ) Zulu
   - Asante sana ( ) Bantu

7. Match the leader (Mansa Musa, Nelson Mandela, Wangari Maathai) with their accomplishment.
   - Mansa Musa ( ) Fought against apartheid
   - Nelson Mandela ( ) Golden pilgrimage to Mecca
   - Wangari Maathai ( ) Founded the Green Belt Movement

8. Match the food (injera, jollof rice, couscous) with the region where it is a staple.
   - Injera ( ) East Africa
   - Jollof rice ( ) West Africa
   - Couscous ( ) North Africa

9. Match the animal (springbok, elephant, lion) with the savanna environment.
   - Springbok ( ) Savanna
   - Elephant ( ) Savanna and other habitats
   - Lion ( ) Savanna and other habitats

10. Match the house style (mudbrick, rondavel, igloo) with the region where it is found.
    - Mudbrick ( ) Sub-Saharan Africa
    - Rondavel ( ) Southern Africa
    - Igloo ( ) Arctic regions

You've reached the end of your exploration of Africa's diverse ethnic groups and traditions. This journey has taken you from the masquerades of West Africa to the intricate beadwork of the Maasai and from the ancient rock art of the Sahara to the philosophy of Ubuntu that binds many African societies together.

The richness of African culture lies not just in its diversity but also in its enduring spirit. These traditions have been passed down through generations, evolving and adapting to changing times. The resilience of these communities and their ability to celebrate their identities while facing challenges is truly inspiring.

Answers

Multiple Choice Answers

1. **A) Djembe** (The djembe, a goblet-shaped drum with a deep sound, is a cornerstone of West African music.)

2. **B) Kuba cloth** (Kuba cloth is known for its geometric patterns and vibrant colors.)

3. **C) The Sahara Desert** (The Sahara Desert, once a lush savanna, is home to a treasure trove of prehistoric rock art.)

4. **D) All of the above** (Masquerade masks represent spirits, ancestors, or mythical figures, blurring the lines between the physical and spiritual realms. They also frighten away evil spirits or represent specific roles in a ceremony.)

5. **C) Textile production** (The indigo-dyed fabrics showcase the artistry and technical skills involved in African textile production.)

6. **C) Infrastructure development and scholarship** (Mansa Musa's reign saw investments in infrastructure projects and support for Islamic scholarship.)

7. **B) Guerilla tactics and alliances** (Queen Nzinga employed guerilla warfare and alliances to defend her people against Portuguese colonialism.)

8. **B) Reconciliation and forgiveness** (Mandela advocated for reconciliation and forgiveness between the races in South Africa after apartheid ended.)

9. **B) Environmental conservation and women's empowerment** (Wangari Maathai's Green Belt Movement addressed environmental degradation through tree planting while empowering women.)

10. **B) West Africa** (The Nok culture, known for its terracotta head sculptures, flourished in what is now Nigeria.)

True or False Answers

1. **True** (The ruins of Great Zimbabwe, a complex of massive stone structures, stand as a testament to the architectural achievements of the ancient Zimbabwean civilization.)

2. **False** (Africa boasts a rich combination of religions and belief systems, with variations existing between and even within ethnic

groups. Some societies practice traditional religions, while others follow Islam, Christianity, or a blend of these faiths.)

3. **True** (Griots, using storytelling, singing, and musical instruments, are repositories of oral history, passing down knowledge, traditions, and cultural values from generation to generation.)

4. **False** (The kola nut, while sometimes enjoyed for its bitter taste, also holds cultural significance in some West African societies, as it is used in ceremonies and as a symbol of hospitality.)

5. **False** (Kente cloth, known for its bold colors and intricate patterns, is traditionally associated with the Ashanti people of West Africa, not the Maasai of East Africa.)

6. **True** (While the beadwork is visually stunning, it also carries cultural significance and can represent social status, wealth, or specific events in a person's life.)

7. **True** (Sundiata Keita's military prowess and diplomatic skills were instrumental in uniting various Mande groups under the banner of the Mali Empire.)

8. **True** (Traditional dance forms in Africa are often expressive and symbolic, conveying stories about history, mythology, or social issues.)

9. **True** (Coming-of-age ceremonies mark an important transition in a person's life, signifying their passage into adulthood and taking on new roles within their community.)

10. **True** (Ubuntu, a philosophy emphasizing interconnectedness, humanity, and respect for others, is a core value in many African societies.)

Fill-in-the-Blank Answers

1. **Ethnic Groups** (Ethnic groups are populations of people who share a common cultural heritage.)

2. **Culture** (Culture encompasses the beliefs, customs, practices, and social behavior of a particular ethnic group.)

3. **Bantu** (The Bantu people are a large language group inhabiting vast swathes of Central, Eastern, and Southern Africa.)

4. **Isolating** and **Unifying** (The Great Rift Valley's geographical isolation has contributed to the diversification of ethnic groups, while its valleys have been migration routes for some groups.)

5. **Sub-Saharan** (Animism is a widespread traditional belief system in Sub-Saharan Africa.)

6. **Oral tradition** (Oral tradition refers to the transmission of knowledge, stories, and history through spoken word.)

7. **Historians** (Griots are keepers of history and culture within their communities.)

8. **Textiles** (Textiles are a prominent art form across Africa, used in clothing, decoration, and ceremonies.)

9. **Muhammad Ali Pasha** (Muhammad Ali Pasha was an Albanian Ottoman ruler who implemented reforms that modernized Egypt's military, economy, and education system.)

10. **Pan-Africanism** (Pan-Africanism is a movement that emphasizes the unity of the African continent and its people.)

One-Word Answers

1. **Nok** (The Nok culture flourished in what is now Nigeria and is known for its distinctive terracotta sculptures, the earliest such art found in Sub-Saharan Africa.)

2. **Kora** (This instrument is known for its beautiful sound and intricate carvings.)

3. **Fulani** (The Fulani people are a nomadic pastoralist ethnic group spread across West Africa.)

4. **Amharic** (Amharic is a Semitic language with a long literary tradition.)

5. **Animism** (The Dogon people have a complex animistic belief system that reveres spirits and ancestors.)

6. **Great Migration** (This spectacular natural event sees millions of wildebeest and zebra traverse the savannas of Kenya and Tanzania.)

7. **Kente** (Kente cloth is a symbol of wealth and cultural significance in West Africa.)

8. **Beadwork** (South African beadwork traditions are diverse and often tell stories or represent social status.)

9. **Eunoto** (This ceremony marks the transition from childhood to adulthood.)

10. **Namib** (The Namib Desert is a coastal desert stretching along the southwestern coast of Africa.)

Quick Fact Match Answers

1. Shaka Zulu/Zulu Kingdom; Cleopatra/Ancient Egypt; Haile Selassie/Ethiopian Empire.

2. Kuba/Kuba cloth; Maasai/Shuka; Ashanti/Kente cloth.

3. Rock art/Paintings; Sculpture/Terracotta (or wood, bronze, etc.); Mask/Wood (or fabric, etc.).

4. Djembe/West Africa; Kora/West Africa (can also be found in Central Africa); Mbira/East Africa and Central Africa.

5. Coming-of-age/Transition into adulthood; Pilgrimage/Journey to a sacred place; Harvest/Celebrating a bountiful harvest.

6. Ubuntu/Zulu; Harambee/Bantu; Asante sana/Swahili (though spoken in many parts of Africa).

7. Mansa Musa/Golden pilgrimage to Mecca; Nelson Mandela/Fought against apartheid; Wangari Maathai/Founded the Green Belt Movement.

8. Injera/East Africa; Jollof rice/West Africa; Couscous/North Africa and parts of West Africa.

9. Springbok/Savanna; Elephant/Savanna and other habitats (forests, grasslands); Lion/Savanna and other habitats (grasslands, woodlands).

10. Mudbrick/Sub-Saharan Africa; Rondavel/Southern Africa; Igloo/Arctic regions.

Chapter 6: The Nile: The Lifeline of Ancient African Civilizations

More than just a river, the Nile has been the lifeblood of civilizations, the cradle of human development, and the backdrop for countless historical narratives. For millennia, its waters have shaped landscapes, influenced cultures, and inspired awe in all who have witnessed its power.

In this chapter, you will explore the fascinating geography and hydrology of the Nile and discover how it played a pivotal role in the rise of four great ancient African empires. You will be amazed by the ingenious techniques communities used to harness its waters – draining fields, constructing pyramids, and building thriving societies.

This chapter is perfect for history enthusiasts and trivia lovers alike. You will uncover the rich history of the Nile, the enduring myths that have surrounded it for centuries, and the extraordinary creatures that call it home.

Ancient and Modern Life Along the Nile

For thousands of years, the Nile River has been central to the lives of the people who have inhabited its valley. From the rise of powerful pharaohs to the development of modern towns, the river's life-giving waters have shaped the social, economic, and cultural evolution of civilizations along its banks. Now, let us explore how the Nile has remained an enduring force, sustaining and intertwining with life from ancient times to the present day.

The Cradle of Agriculture:

- **Fertile Fields:** Every year, the Nile floods dump rich, fertile silt onto the land, creating a natural irrigation that is perfect for agriculture. This reliable cycle allowed the Egyptians and other civilizations to grow crops such as wheat, barley, and vegetables, sustaining huge communities and kick-starting settled societies.

- **Engineering Marvels:** Ancient civilizations further harnessed the bounties of the Nile in the elaborate construction of canals and irrigation systems. Such engineering exploits constantly assured a stream of water to the fields ensuring forefront agricultural productivity.

- **Modern Techniques:** Today, modern irrigation techniques have replaced many ancient canals, but the Nile is still the lifeblood of much of the agriculture in the region. Cotton, sugarcane, and rice are just a few main crops grown along the Nile Valley, which feed millions and greatly contribute to the economies of Egypt and other Nile Basin countries.

A Highway of Commerce:

- **The Old Traffic:** Besides being a source of water, the Nile was a significant transportation route. Boatmen transported passengers, goods, and ideas along the river from one settlement to another. This transport system facilitated trade between regional Egypt and beyond, which would usher in cultural exchange and the consequent economic prosperity.

- **Modern Transport:** While the passage of goods by land is now mostly by motorcar and truck, in the past, the Nile clearly had more vital importance as a watercourse. Once loaded with cargo, barges float downstream for long distances between towns and ports along the river. The tourism trade floats around another type of vessel in the Nile – the cruise ship – taking tourists on board to show them some perspicacity into an ancient civilization and the beauty of its landscape.

Cultural and Religious Meaning:

- **The River of Gods:** Awe and yearning were in the hearts of the ancient civilization for the Nile, with its life-sustaining qualities and yearly cycle of inundation. The river was considered a deity amongst several ancient societies along its course, with its role being painted extensively in their mythologies, legends, and religious beliefs.

- **Festivals and Traditions:** The Nile flood planted the seeds of jubilant celebration, marking the onset of the planting season that heralded life anew. Festivals and rites handed down from the Nile continue in parts of the region, connecting its peoples to their ancestry and the river's full circle of life.

- **A Common Cause:** No other river creates ties that connect nationalities. The Nile serves as a common resource that connects the lives and fates of millions of people within several African countries. Cooperation and dialogue in managing the water resources are thus indispensable to ensure the welfare of all those who depend on it.

The river is a story about a resilient and adaptable life, one closely linked to humanity's relationship with nature. For centuries, the Nile has provided a source of subsistence, a highway for communication, and an emotional stream spanning much of the spectrum of cultural expression. The sustainable management of this critical resource will, in the coming decades, be a key to ensuring the development of a vibrant future for the Nile Valley's communities.

Engineering Marvels of the Nile

Aside from the river influencing developments there, the Nile has been receptive to amazing feats of engineering by humanity. While ancient irrigation systems have watered farmlands, it is the Aswan Dam that has gained wide recognition in modern times and showcases the ingenuity of those who dwelt along the banks of the Nile.

The Ancient Wonders:

- **Irrigation systems:** The Nile's annual flooding is, and has always been a double-edged sword. While the fertile soil deposited by the Nile was an asset, the floods also could prove to be destructive. Hence, ancient civilizations such as the Egyptians developed elaborate networks of irrigation to control the flow of the Nile. Canals, dikes, and basins were painstakingly fashioned so as to divert water into fields, ensuring a continuous supply of crops throughout the year. The shadoof-a simple lever system using buckets- was also employed to lift the river's water into higher fields.

- **The Pyramid Construction:** The pyramid of Giza, a monumental tomb for pharaohs, bears witness to the engineering creativity of the ancient Egyptians. Such massive edifices, raised by millions of accurately cut stones, would require a profound knowledge of geometry, weight distribution, and logistics. The ensemble effort and ingenuity needed to transport these massive stones-most likely via ramps using water channels-are further evidence of human ingenuity.

Modern Engineering:

- **The Aswan High Dam:** This huge dam regulates the waters of the Nile River so that it does not flood into the areas around southern Egypt. The mighty Aswan High Dam, built in the years of 1970, will regulate the flow of the Nile River in such ways as to prevent the destructive floods that once plagued the region and provide water for irrigation and hydroelectricity. Naturally, the project is considered to undoubtedly involve the forced relocation of populations and disruptions to the Nile itself.

- **Modern irrigation systems:** While ancient irrigation systems laid the ground, modern technology enhanced their management of the Nile. Canals have been lined with concrete to prevent water loss, and electric-powered pumps work with traditional methods to ensure an effective water supply.

A Legacy of Ingenuity:

Both ancient and modern engineering marvels along the Nile highlight humanity's remarkable ability to understand and adapt to the natural world. The river's massive floods, vast expanses, and other challenges drove the development of innovative technologies that continue to shape life along its banks. By studying these ancient achievements, we gain insight into the advanced knowledge of past societies and their ability to undertake the immense task of sustainably harnessing the Nile's resources.

Multiple Choice

Explore your understanding of the Nile River's role in shaping African history with these multiple-choice questions.

1. Which ancient civilization developed along the banks of the Nile River?

   A) Egyptian

   B) Ghanaian

   C) Zulu

   D) Aztec

2. The annual flooding of the Nile created fertile fields by depositing what on the land?

   A) Fine sand

   B) Rich silt

   C) Clay

   D) All of the above

3. Shadoofs were simple lever systems used in ancient Egypt for what purpose?

   A) Transporting large stones

   B) Raising water from the Nile for irrigation

   C) Carving hieroglyphs

   D) Building pyramids

4. The Aswan High Dam, a modern marvel of engineering on the Nile River, is primarily used for what purposes?

   A) Flood control and generating electricity

   B) Navigation and recreation

   C) Building new cities

   D) Mining precious metals

5. What natural wonder is the annual flooding cycle of the Nile River most associated with?

   A) The Great Rift Valley

   B) The Sahara Desert

   C) The Red Sea

   D) The Fertile Nile Delta

6. Canals, dikes, and basins were all part of what complex system developed by ancient civilizations to manage the Nile's flow?

    A) Pyramid construction techniques

    B) Hieroglyphic writing system

    C) Ancient irrigation systems

    D) Trade routes along the Nile

7. The intricate carvings and hieroglyphs adorning the walls of ancient Egyptian temples were often created from what type of stone, readily available near the Nile?

    A) Granite

    B) Sandstone

    C) Marble

    D) Volcanic rock

8. Cruise ships navigating the Nile River today offer tourists a glimpse into what, besides the beautiful scenery?

    A) The bustling modern cities along the Nile

    B) The fascinating wildlife of the Nile Delta

    C) The grandeur of ancient civilizations

    D) The traditional fishing practices on the Nile

9. The sustainable management of the Nile's water resources is crucial for what reason?

    A) Maintaining the tourism industry

    B) Ensuring the well-being of millions who depend on the Nile

    C) Preventing the construction of new dams

    D) Encouraging international trade

10. The Nile River is often referred to as the "lifeline" of ancient African civilizations because of its role in:

    A) Military defense and transportation

    B) Monument construction and religious beliefs

    C) All of the above

    D) None of the above

True or False

Distinguish fact from fiction with these statements about the Nile River's historical significance.

1. The Nile River flows from south to north.
   - o True
   - o False

2. The annual flooding of the Nile River was a completely unpredictable event that caused devastation.
   - o True
   - o False

3. Shadoofs were complex machines used by ancient Egyptians to transport massive stones for pyramid construction.
   - o True
   - o False

4. While providing benefits, the Aswan High Dam has also displaced communities and impacted the Nile's ecosystem.
   - o True
   - o False

5. The intricate pyramids of Giza were built using only basic tools and human labor.
   - o True
   - o False

6. Canals, dikes, and basins were all part of a sophisticated irrigation network developed by ancient civilizations to manage the Nile's waters.
   - o True
   - o False

7. The fertile soil deposited by the Nile floods was ideal for growing wheat, barley, and vegetables.
   - o True
   - o False

8. Cruise ships navigating the Nile today offer tourists a chance to experience the bustling modern cities along the riverbanks.
   o True
   o False

9. The sustainable management of the Nile's water resources is a critical concern for several African countries that depend on the river.
   o True
   o False

10. The ancient Egyptians believed the Nile to be a divine entity and incorporated it into their mythology and religious practices.
    o True
    o False

Fill in the Blank

1. The source of the Nile River is located in the mountains of _____.

2. The Nile River flows _____, eventually emptying into the Mediterranean Sea.

3. The annual flooding of the Nile deposited fertile _____ along the riverbanks, ideal for agriculture.

4. _____ was the earliest civilization to develop along the Nile River.

5. The Egyptians worshiped the Nile god _____, who they believed was responsible for the annual floods.

6. The papyrus plant, which grew abundantly along the Nile, was used by the Egyptians to create a form of writing material called _____.

7. The Great Pyramids of Giza are located near the city of _____ in Egypt.

8. The massive stone statues known as sphinxes are found guarding the entrance to _____ in Egypt.

9. The _____ is a famous ancient temple complex on the Nile's banks.

10. The Kush civilization, a rival kingdom to Egypt, flourished along the southern reaches of the Nile River in what is now modern-day _____.

One-Word Answer Questions

Test your knowledge of the Nile River, the lifeblood of ancient African civilizations. Here are ten one-word answer questions to see how much you remember about this fascinating river and its impact.

1. What is the name of the longest river in the world?
   Response: _____.

2. What sea does the Nile River empty into?
   Response: _____.

3. Which modern-day country is the source of the Blue Nile?
   Response: _____.

4. What massive lake does the White Nile flow through?
   Response: _____.

5. What fertile region was created by the annual flooding of the Nile?
   Response: _____.

6. What crop grown in the Nile Valley was a staple food source for ancient Egyptians?
   Response: _____.

7. What building material was abundant in the Nile Valley and used to construct pyramids?
   Response: _____.

8. What famous Egyptian pharaoh was buried in the Great Pyramid of Giza?
   Response: _____.

9. What god did the ancient Egyptians associate with the Nile River?
   Response: _____.

10. What modern-day city is located at the northern delta of the Nile River?

Response: _____.

Quick Fact Match

Test your knowledge by matching these Nile-related facts.

1. Match the city with its location relative to the Nile River.
   - Cairo ( ) South
   - Luxor ( ) North
   - Khartoum ( ) East

2. Match the term with its definition.
   - Shadoof ( ) The annual flooding of the Nile River
   - Inundation ( ) The writing system of ancient Egypt
   - Hieroglyphics ( ) A simple irrigation tool

3. Match the structure with its historical period.
   - Pyramid ( ) Millions of years ago
   - Aswan High Dam ( ) Ancient Egypt
   - Great Rift Valley ( ) 20th century

4. Match the benefit with the aspect of the Nile River.
   - Flood control ( ) The annual flooding
   - Transportation ( ) The Aswan High Dam
   - Fertile soil ( ) The Nile River itself

5. Match the modern activity with the ancient practice to which it relates.
   - Farming ( ) Trade and travel on the Nile
   - Cruising ( ) Building pyramids
   - Excavating ( ) Ancient irrigation systems

6. Match the material with its use in ancient Egypt.
   o Granite ( ) Writing material
   o Papyrus ( ) Temples and tombs
   o Sandstone ( ) Statues and sarcophagi

7. Match the environmental concern with the potential impact of the Aswan High Dam.
   o Water scarcity ( ) Less fertile silt deposition
   o Soil erosion ( ) Increased salt concentration in the soil
   o Salinization ( ) Reduced water flow downstream

8. Match the god/goddess with their association with ancient Egyptian religion.
   o Osiris ( ) Love, beauty, and motherhood
   o Hathor ( ) Sun god and creator
   o Ra ( ) Underworld and rebirth
   o

9. Match the achievement with the ancient civilization.
   o Building the Pyramids ( ) Multiple Nile Valley civilizations
   o Developing irrigation systems ( ) Ancient Egypt
   o Mummification ( ) Ancient Egypt

10. Match the natural wonder with its location relative to the Nile River.
    o Sahara Desert ( ) Northernmost point of the Nile
    o Nile Delta ( ) West of the Nile
    o Great Rift Valley ( ) Eastern part of Nile

The journey down the Nile River has come to an end, but the story of this remarkable waterway continues to unfold. From the ingenuity of ancient civilizations who harnessed their power to the challenges and opportunities of modern times, the Nile River remains a vital force in shaping the lives of millions.

This chapter has explored the Nile's multifaceted role. You've marveled at the engineering feats that tamed its floods and nurtured fertile fields. You've pondered the myths and religious significance that imbued the Nile with a sense of awe. You've also considered the delicate balance of managing a shared resource for the well-being of future generations. By understanding its past and present, you can contribute to a future where this life-giving river continues to nourish the land and the people who call it home.

Answers

Multiple Choice Answers

1. **A) Egyptian** (The ancient Egyptian civilization flourished along the banks of the Nile River.)

2. **D) All of the above** (The annual flooding deposited fertile silt, fine sand, and clay, enriching the land for agriculture.)

3. **B) Raising water from the Nile for irrigation** (Shadoofs were a simple but effective irrigation tool.)

4. **A) Flood control and generating electricity** (The Aswan High Dam regulates the Nile's flow and generates hydroelectric power.)

5. **D) The Fertile Crescent** (The concept of a fertile region due to predictable flooding is similar to the Fertile Crescent in Mesopotamia, although not geographically connected.)

6. **C) Ancient irrigation systems** (These complex systems ensured efficient water management for agriculture.)

7. **B) Sandstone** (Sandstone, a readily-available stone near the Nile, was widely used in ancient Egyptian construction.)

8. **C) The grandeur of ancient civilizations** (Cruise ships offer a glimpse into the remarkable achievements of ancient societies along the Nile.)

9. **B) Ensuring the well-being of millions who depend on the Nile** (Sustainable water management is vital for agriculture, drinking water, and the environment.)

10. **C) All of the above** (The Nile's role encompassed agriculture, transportation, construction, and religious beliefs.)

True or False Answers

1. **True.** The Nile River famously flows northward from its source in East Africa to its delta on the Mediterranean Sea.

2. **False.** While the floods were powerful, their timing was predictable, allowing civilizations to plan accordingly.

3. **False.** Shadoofs were simple lever systems used for irrigation, not transporting massive stones.

4. **True.** The dam's construction had both positive and negative consequences.

5. **False.** While the ingenuity of the builders is undeniable, they likely used ramps, rollers, and waterways to move the stones.

6. **True.** This complex irrigation system ensured a steady water supply for agriculture.

7. **True.** The rich silt created fertile land perfect for sustaining a robust agricultural society.

8. **False.** While some cities exist along the Nile, the focus of these cruises is on the natural beauty and historical sites.

9. **True.** Cooperation between Nile Basin countries is essential for ensuring water security for all.

10. **True.** The Nile's life-giving properties inspired reverence, and it played a significant role in Egyptian mythology.

Fill-in-the-Blank Answers

1. **East Africa** (The source of the Nile is Lake Victoria in the mountains of Rwanda, Burundi, and Uganda).

2. **Northward** (The Nile River flows northward through several countries before reaching the Mediterranean Sea).

3. **Silt** (The annual floods deposited rich, fertile silt along the Nile's banks, creating ideal conditions for growing crops).

4. **Ancient Egyptians** (The Ancient Egyptians were one of the earliest civilizations to develop along the Nile River, around 3100 BCE).

5. **Hapy** (Hapy was the Egyptian god of the Nile floods, who was believed to bring life and prosperity to the land).

6. **Papyrus** (The Egyptians used Papyrus reeds to create papyrus, a form of paper-like writing material).

7. **Cairo** (The Great Pyramids of Giza are located on the Giza Plateau near Cairo, Egypt).

8. **Temples** (Sphinxes are statues with the body of a lion and the head of a human or a mythical creature. They were often placed guarding the entrances to temples).

9. **Luxor Temple** (The Luxor Temple is a large and impressive temple complex located on the east bank of the Nile River in the city of Luxor).

10. **Sudan** (The Kush civilization was a powerful kingdom located along the southern Nile River in what is now modern-day Sudan).

One-Word Answers

1. **Nile** (The Nile River is the longest river in the world, stretching over 6,650 kilometers (4,132 miles) from East Africa to the Mediterranean Sea.)

2. **Mediterranean** (The Nile River empties into the Mediterranean Sea, providing a vital source of water and transportation for civilizations throughout history.)

3. **Ethiopia** (The Blue Nile originates in the Ethiopian highlands and contributes significantly to the annual flooding of the Nile.)

4. **Lake Victoria** (The White Nile, the longest tributary of the Nile, flows through the vast Lake Victoria in East Africa.)

5. **Nile Delta** (The annual flooding of the Nile deposited rich, fertile soil along the river valley, known as the Nile Delta, which was ideal for agriculture.)

6. **Wheat** (Wheat was a major crop grown in the fertile Nile Valley and provided sustenance for the ancient Egyptians.)

7. **Stone** (Stone, particularly limestone, was abundant in the Nile Valley and used extensively in the construction of pyramids and temples.)

8. **Khufu** (or Cheops) (Khufu was the pharaoh believed to have commissioned the construction of the Great Pyramid of Giza.)

9. **Hapi** (The ancient Egyptians worshiped Hapi, the god of the Nile floods, who they believed ensured the fertility of their land.)

10. **Cairo** (Cairo, the capital of Egypt, is situated near the northern delta of the Nile River, where the river branches out before emptying into the Mediterranean Sea.)

Quick Fact Match Answers

1. Cairo/North; Luxor/East; Khartoum/South.

2. Shadoof/A simple irrigation tool; Inundation/The annual flooding of the Nile River; Hieroglyphics/The writing system of ancient Egypt.

3. Pyramid/Ancient Egypt; Aswan High Dam/20th century; Great Rift Valley/Millions of years ago.

4. Flood control/The Aswan High Dam; Transportation/The Nile River itself; Fertile soil/The annual flooding.

5. Farming/Ancient irrigation systems; Cruising/Trade and travel on the Nile; Excavating/Building pyramids.

6. Granite/Statues and sarcophagi; Papyrus/Writing material; Sandstone/Temples and tombs.

7. Water scarcity/Reduced water flow downstream; Soil erosion/Less fertile silt deposition; Salinization/Increased salt concentration in the soil.

8. Osiris/Underworld and rebirth; Hathor/Love, beauty, and motherhood; Ra/Sun god and creator.

9. Building the Pyramids/Ancient Egypt; Developing irrigation systems/Multiple Nile Valley civilizations; Mummification/Ancient Egypt.

10. Sahara Desert/East of the Nile; Nile Delta/Northernmost point of the Nile; Great Rift Valley/South of the Nile.

Chapter 7: The Scramble for Africa and Its Impact

Africa's history, beyond its pre-modern empires and great rivers, is marked by a recurring cycle of upheaval driven by both internal and external forces. This chapter examines one such pivotal moment, now widely known as "The Scramble for Africa,"—a period of intense European colonization.

The term *Scramble* itself carries powerful connotations, evoking an era of aggressive competition as multiple European powers vied for control over African territories. While the motivations behind colonization were complex and often debated, its consequences remain undeniable. This chapter will explore the driving forces behind the Scramble, the methods of conquest employed by European nations, and the lasting imprint it left on African societies, cultures, and political systems.

Understanding this period requires recognizing its fragility and complexity. Colonial rule was often brutal and exploitative, leaving behind deep-rooted social and economic inequalities that persist today. This chapter aims to provide an objective examination, considering perspectives from both the colonizers and the colonized. A critical analysis of this era offers valuable insight into the forces that shaped modern Africa.

Colonial Impact on Africa

The "Scramble for Africa" was the period of aggressive competition in European colonization of Africa roughly between the end of the 19th century and the beginning of the 20th century. The consequences of this contest would have grave, lasting impacts on the continent.

Causes of Colonization:

The motives behind European colonization, therefore, were complex and layered. These include, among other factors, the following:

- **Economic Factors:** European powers were eager to get into Africa to exploit its vast mineral, timber, and ivory resources. Colonization often provided access to those resources, along with new markets for European commodities.

- **Strategic Considerations:** They would provide a strategic advantage to Europe with respect to global trade and military competition, especially with respect to ports and coaling stations along the lines of communication.

- **Social Darwinism:** Many Europeans held a view that their race and culture were superior and used this view to justify colonization as a civilizing mission. Nationalism also aroused the desire for empire-building and global dominance.

Diversity of Colonial Powers:

The competition in Africa involved a number of European powers, each of whose methods and goals differed. Key players involved:

- **Britain:** The colonies were Nigeria, Kenya, and South Africa. They emphasized resource extraction and settler colonies in certain regions.

- **France:** French colonies extended across West and Central Africa. They strove to rigidly assimilate these African colonies into a French economic and political system.

- **Germany:** German colonies were Namibia and Tanzania; their rule was often tyrannical, with a clear policy of resource extraction.

- **Belgium:** King Leopold II's rule of the Congo Free State provides one of the most ghastly illustrations of colonial exploitation.

- **Portugal:** Portugal had long been interested in maintaining colonies in Africa, with these being Angola and Mozambique.

Impact of Colonialism:

The legacy of European colonization of Africa still reverberates today. Here are some key points:

- **Political Fragmentation:** European powers arbitrarily drew boundaries, ignoring ethnic and cultural boundaries; this would lead to future wars and conflicts within the newly formed African countries.

- **Complete Scavenging:** Economies were seen as a source of raw materials and support for that, so the infrastructure development in these colonies was, at best, minimal.

- **Disruption of Social Orders:** Societies that had existed for thousands of years were repeatedly undermined; ethnic unrest and loss of cultural identity ensued.

- **Resistance and National Independence:** This culminated in independence movements that changed the political landscape entirely.

Transformational Legacy:

The complex and multi-layered legacy of colonization is being experienced during the journey to independence. Yes, amidst the exploitation and violence, it cannot be denied that this process brought change to the continent.

The colonial infrastructure – schools, hospitals, roads, railroads, and guns – helped build nations in Africa.

Knowing and understanding the period is key to fully grasping the current nature of most opportunities and threats/intrusions happening all over Africa. It's a story of resilience, resistance, and an endless quest for self-sufficiency.

African Resistance and Liberation Movements

The era of European colonization in Africa was not met with passive acceptance. Throughout the continent, a spirit of resistance burned bright. This section explores the diverse forms of resistance and the rise of liberation movements that ultimately led to African independence.

Early Forms of Resistance:

Colonial rule was never met with silence – resistance was widespread and vibrant across the African continent long before European dominance was fully established. This chapter explores the diverse forms of resistance, from localized uprisings to prolonged struggles that spanned over a century. Many of these movements ultimately paved the way for Africa's independence, highlighting the resilience and determination of its people.

Early Resistance:

- **Military Resistance:** Many (and often subnational) elements of resistance lashed out against colonization with wars: heroic resistance of the Asante Kings in Ghana to brave Samuel Crowther's commanders in West Africa. The most visible response to colonization was war.

- **Economic Resistance:** Africans who turned to economic strategies against colonialists. With run-off in respective plantations, they searched for other markets and sustenance within local markets.

- **Culture Resistance:** The conservation of traditional languages, religions, and customs was a memorable form of opposition against the systematic annexation of some colonial nations.

Rise of Liberation Movements:

The 20th century saw the rise of organized liberation movements across Africa. These movements, inspired by ideals of self-determination and Pan-Africanism, employed various strategies to achieve independence.

- **Notable Leaders:**
  - **Kwame Nkrumah of Ghana:** A charismatic leader who spearheaded Ghana's independence movement and became the country's first president.

- o **Nelson Mandela of South Africa:** An iconic figure in the fight against apartheid, Mandela spent 27 years in prison before leading South Africa to democratic elections.
- o **Jomo Kenyatta of Kenya:** A leading figure in Kenya's independence movement who became the country's first president.
- o **Patrice Lumumba of the Democratic Republic of the Congo:** A prominent leader who advocated for a unified and independent Congo but was assassinated during a period of political turmoil.

- **Strategies for Liberation:** These movements employed diverse strategies, including:
  - o **Peaceful Protests:** Boycotts, strikes, and non-violent demonstrations were used to raise awareness and pressure colonial powers.
  - o **Armed Struggle:** In some cases, armed resistance movements fought against colonial forces.
  - o **Political Lobbying:** African leaders sought international support for independence movements at the United Nations and through diplomatic channels.

The Road to Independence:

It was a long and hard struggle. But through perseverance and many people's dedication, African nations eventually got free. Here are some key dates:

- **Ghana:** Ghana, formerly the Gold Coast, was the first sub-Saharan African country to get free in 1957 with Kwame Nkrumah.
- **The 1960s:** The 1960s was the year of Africa. Many French and British colonies became free during this period.
- **Southern Africa:** The struggle for liberation in Southern Africa, particularly against apartheid in South Africa, continued until the late 20th century. Nelson Mandela's release from prison in 1990 and the eventual collapse of apartheid was a big win for the liberation movement. The release of Mandela from prison in 1990 and the fall of apartheid became major victories for the liberation movement.

A Legacy of Toughness:

The tale of African resistance and liberation movements is proof of the continent's mettle. Even though some colonialists were notoriously brutal, the fight for freedom never left. These movements took years of independence struggles and the passing of tests for the establishment of democratic institutions and the enhancement of pan-African identity.

It was not always easy sailing, and the legacy of colonialism still informs African politics today. But the bravery and determination of those who fought for freedom have inspired the next generation.

Multiple Choice

Examine your understanding of the European colonization of Africa and its lasting influence with these multiple-choice questions.

1. Which European country colonized Kenya and Zimbabwe?

    A) France

    B) Britain

    C) Portugal

2. The "Scramble for Africa" refers to the period of intense competition among European powers to:

    A) Establish trade partnerships with African nations.

    B) Spread Christianity throughout the continent.

    C) Claim and control African territories.

    D) Promote cultural exchange between Europe and Africa.

3. A key motive for European colonization of Africa was the desire to gain access to:

    A) Advanced educational systems in Africa.

    B) Africa's vast resources like minerals and timber.

    C) Established trade routes within Africa.

    D) Religious pilgrimage sites in Africa.

4. The concept of Social Darwinism, used by some Europeans to justify colonization, emphasized the following:

    A) Importance of cultural exchange and mutual understanding.

    B) Equality and shared prosperity between Europe and Africa.

    C) Superiority of the European race and culture.

    D) Importance of preserving traditional African societies.

5. Which of the following was NOT a major European colonial power in Africa?

   A) Germany

   B) Italy

   C) Austria

   D) Britain

6. The arbitrary borders drawn by European powers during colonization often:

   A) United different ethnic groups under one government.

   B) Followed natural geographic boundaries like rivers and mountains.

   C) Disregarded ethnic and cultural identities, leading to future conflicts.

   D) Promoted economic cooperation between different African regions.

7. Resistance to colonial rule in Africa took many forms, including:

   A) Only military uprisings against European forces.

   B) A variety of methods like military resistance, economic tactics, and cultural preservation.

   C) Primarily peaceful protests and demonstrations.

   D) Collaboration with European powers to maintain control.

8. Kwame Nkrumah was a prominent leader in the independence movement of:

   A) Nigeria

   B) South Africa

   C) Ghana

   D) Kenya

9. The dismantling of apartheid in South Africa marked a significant victory for the:

   A) European colonial administration.

   B) Ideals of racial segregation and white dominance.

   C) African liberation movement fighting for equality.

   D) Continued economic dependence of South Africa on Europe.

10. Understanding the era of colonialism in Africa is crucial because it:

   A) Has no lasting impact on the continent today.

   B) Provides valuable insights into the challenges and opportunities faced by Africa.

   C) Only glorifies the achievements of European powers.

   D) Is a historical footnote irrelevant to modern Africa.

True or False

Distinguish fact from fiction with these statements about the European colonization of Africa and its lasting influence.

1. European powers colonized all African countries.

   o True

   o False

2. The "Scramble for Africa" refers to a period of peaceful cooperation between European nations regarding trade with Africa.

   o True

   o False

3. European motivations for colonization of Africa solely focused on spreading Christianity.

   o True

   o False

4. Social Darwinism, a belief system used by some Europeans, emphasized the importance of cultural exchange and mutual understanding.

   o True

   o False

5. King Leopold II of Belgium is remembered for his fair and just rule of the Congo Free State.

   o True

   o False

6. The arbitrary borders drawn by European powers during colonization often contributed to future conflicts within newly formed African nations.

   o True

   o False

7. Resistance to colonial rule in Africa was limited to military uprisings against European forces.

   o True

   o False

8. Nelson Mandela was a key figure in the fight against apartheid in South Africa.

   o True

   o False

9. The dismantling of apartheid in South Africa marked the end of all racial tensions in the country.

   o True

   o False

10. Understanding the era of colonialism in Africa is irrelevant to comprehending the continent's contemporary challenges and opportunities.

    o True

    o False

Fill in the Blank

Test your memory of the era of European colonization and its lasting impact on Africa.

1. The _____ refers to the period of intense competition among European powers to claim territories in Africa.

2. European motivations for colonization included access to Africa's vast resources and new markets for their _____.

3. Some Europeans used the concept of _____ to justify colonization, emphasizing the superiority of the European race and culture.

4. European powers often drew _____ borders during colonization, disregarding ethnic and cultural identities.

5. _____ resistance to colonial rule took many forms, including military uprisings, economic tactics, and cultural preservation.

6. Kwame Nkrumah was a prominent leader in the independence movement of _____.

7. Nelson Mandela was a key figure in the fight against apartheid in _____.

8. The dismantling of apartheid in South Africa marked a significant victory for the _____ movement.

9. Understanding the era of colonialism is crucial because it provides insights into the challenges and _____ faced by Africa today.

10. The legacy of colonialism in Africa is complex, with both positive and _____ consequences.

One-Word Answer Questions

Test your knowledge of the key terms and figures associated with European colonization and its impact on Africa. Answer in just one word.

1. Name the West African country that was first to gain independence in 1957.

   Response: _____.

2. What was the period of intense competition among European powers to claim African territories called?

   Response: _____.

3. What economic theory used by some Europeans justified colonization based on racial superiority?

   Response: _____.

4. What type of borders drawn by European powers often disregarded ethnic and cultural identities?

   Response: _____.

5. What was a general term for the movements fighting for independence from European rule in Africa?

   Response: _____.

6. Kwame Nkrumah was a prominent leader in the independence movement of what modern-day country?

   Response: _____.

7. Nelson Mandela was a key figure in the dismantling of what system of racial segregation in South Africa?

   Response: _____.

8. What was a significant consequence of colonialism for many African nations?

   Response: _____.

9. Understanding the era of colonialism is important because it sheds light on what aspects of Africa today?

   Response: _____.

10. The legacy of colonialism in Africa is complex, with both positive and negative effects. Give a one-word answer for the negative effects.

    Response: _____.

Quick Fact Match

Match the following historical events with the years they are associated with. Write the corresponding letter in the blank.

1. **Match the year with a significant event in African decolonization.**

   A) 1960 ( ) Independence of 17 African nations

   B) 1974 ( ) End of the Angolan War of Independence

   C) 1994 ( ) Dismantling of apartheid in South Africa

2. **Match the leader with the country's independence movement they led.**

   A) Kwame Nkrumah ( ) Kenya

   B) Jomo Kenyatta ( ) Ghana

   C) Nelson Mandela ( ) South Africa

3. **Match the European nation with its African colony.**

   A) France ( ) Nigeria

   B) Britain ( ) Algeria

   C) Portugal ( ) Angola

4. **Match the term with its definition.**

   A) Scramble for Africa ( ) Period of intense competition for African colonies

   B) Apartheid ( ) System of racial segregation in South Africa

   C) Liberation Movements ( ) Groups fighting for independence from colonial rule

5. **Match the impact of colonialism with its description.**

   A) Political Fragmentation ( ) Arbitrary borders causing future conflicts

   B) Economic Exploitation ( ) Focus on resource extraction, neglecting local development

   C) Cultural Disruption ( ) Loss of traditional practices and identities

6. **Match the invention with its impact on European exploration of Africa.**

   A) Compass ( ) Improved navigation and long-distance travel

   B) Quinine ( ) Treatment for malaria, reducing disease risk

   C) Steamboat ( ) Increased travel on African rivers

7. Match the cash crop with the colonial power associated with its production.

   A) Coffee ( ) France

   B) Cotton ( ) Britain

   C) Rubber ( ) Belgium

8. Match the geographic feature with its role in European colonization.

   A) Mountains ( ) Natural barriers limiting exploration

   B) Rivers ( ) Transportation routes for trade and exploration

   C) Deserts ( ) Impassable barriers to European expansion

9. Match the term with its description.

   A) Pan-Africanism ( ) Movement for unity and cooperation among African nations

   B) Social Darwinism ( ) Theory used to justify European dominance

   C) Assimilation ( ) Policy of forcing Africans to adopt European culture

10. Match the legacy of colonialism with its impact.

   A) Infrastructure Development ( ) Introduction of transportation networks

   B) Educational Systems ( ) Provided access to Western knowledge but may have neglected traditional education

   C) Environmental Degradation ( ) Unsustainable resource use for colonial gain

The journey through the era of European colonization in Africa has been complex and multifaceted. You've explored the motives that fueled the "Scramble for Africa," the methods employed by European powers, and the lasting impact on the continent.

This period was not a static chapter in African history. It was a time of resistance, resilience, and, ultimately, the rise of independent African nations. The legacy of colonialism is a double-edged sword. It left behind infrastructure, education systems, and exposure to new ideas. However, it also resulted in political fragmentation, economic exploitation, and the erosion of traditional cultures.

As you move forward, understanding this period is crucial. The challenges faced by Africa today are deeply rooted in its colonial past. Boundary disputes, resource management issues, and the struggle for economic development all have echoes of the colonial era. However, Africa is not defined by its past. It is a continent brimming with potential, a land of vibrant cultures, and a people determined to shape their destiny. The future of Africa is being written now by its citizens, entrepreneurs, artists, and leaders.

Answers

Multiple Choice Answers

1. **B) Britain** (Britain colonized both Kenya and Zimbabwe.)

2. **C) Claim and control African territories** (The Scramble for Africa was about acquiring colonies and resources.)

3. **B) Africa's vast resources, such as minerals and timber** (Resources were a key motivator for European colonization.)

4. **C) Superiority of the European race and culture** (Social Darwinism was used to justify colonial dominance.)

5. **C) Belgium** (Belgium was a major colonial power, not Austria.)

6. **C) Disregarded ethnic and cultural identities, leading to future conflicts** (Arbitrary borders caused tensions.)

7. **B) A variety of methods like military resistance, economic tactics, and cultural preservation** (Resistance took many forms.)

8. **C) Ghana** (Kwame Nkrumah led Ghana's independence movement.)

9. **C) African liberation movement fighting for equality** (Apartheid's dismantling was a victory for African liberation.)

10. **B) Provides valuable insights into the challenges and opportunities faced by Africa** (Colonialism's legacy is still relevant.)

True or False Answers

1. **False** (Several African countries, like Ethiopia and Liberia, maintained their independence throughout the colonial era.)

2. **False** (The "Scramble for Africa" was a period of intense competition for colonies.)

3. **False** (While religion played a role, economic gain and strategic advantage were also key motives.)

4. **False** (Social Darwinism was used to justify European dominance based on a supposed racial and cultural superiority.)

5. **False** (King Leopold II's rule was marked by brutality and exploitation.)

6. **True** (Disregarding ethnic and cultural identities when drawing borders created tensions.)

7. **False** (The resistance included economic tactics, cultural preservation, and military action.)

8. **True** (Nelson Mandela was a prominent leader in the anti-apartheid movement.)

9. **False** (Dismantling apartheid was a crucial step, but racial issues persist.)

10. **False** (Understanding colonialism sheds light on Africa's development and ongoing challenges.)

Fill-in-the-Blank Answers

1. The **Scramble for Africa** refers to the period of intense competition among European powers to claim territories in Africa.

2. European motivations for colonization included access to Africa's vast resources and new markets for their **goods**.

3. **Social Darwinism**, a concept used by some Europeans to justify colonization, emphasized the superiority of the European race and culture.

4. **Arbitrary** borders were often drawn during colonization, disregarding ethnic and cultural identities.

5. **African** resistance to colonial rule took many forms.

6. Kwame Nkrumah was a prominent leader in the independence movement of **Ghana**.

7. Nelson Mandela was a key figure in the fight against apartheid in **South Africa**.

8. The dismantling of apartheid in South Africa marked a significant victory for the **African liberation** movement.

9. Understanding the era of colonialism is crucial because it provides insights into the challenges and **opportunities** faced by Africa today.

10. The legacy of colonialism in Africa is complex, with both positive and **negative** consequences.

One-Word Answers

1. **Ghana**

2. **Scramble** (The Scramble for Africa)

3. **Darwinism** (Social Darwinism)

4. **Arbitrary**

5. Liberation (Liberation movements)
6. Ghana
7. Apartheid
8. Fragmentation (Political fragmentation)
9. Challenges (or Opportunities)
10. Exploitation

Quick Fact Match Answers

1. 1960/Independence of 17 African nations; 1974/End of the Angolan War of Independence (This event did not mark Angolan independence, which occurred in 1975); 1994/Dismantling of apartheid in South Africa.
2. Kwame Nkrumah/Ghana; Jomo Kenyatta/Kenya; Nelson Mandela/South Africa.
3. France/Algeria; Britain/Nigeria; Portugal/Angola.
4. Scramble for Africa/Period of intense competition for African colonies; Apartheid/System of racial segregation in South Africa; Liberation Movements/Groups fighting for independence from colonial rule.
5. Political Fragmentation/Arbitrary borders causing future conflicts; Economic Exploitation/Focus on resource extraction neglecting local development; Cultural Disruption/Loss of traditional practices and identities.
6. Compass/Improved navigation and long-distance travel; Quinine/Treatment for malaria, reducing disease risk; Steamboat/Increased travel on African rivers.
7. Coffee/France; Cotton/Britain; Rubber/Belgium.
8. Mountains/Natural barriers limiting exploration; Rivers/Transportation routes for trade and exploration; Deserts/Impassable barriers to European expansion (Deserts were obstacles, but not entirely impassable).
9. Pan-Africanism/Movement for unity and cooperation among African nations; Social Darwinism/Theory used to justify European dominance; Assimilation/Policy of forcing Africans to adopt European culture.

10. Infrastructure Development/Introduction of transportation networks; Educational Systems/Provided access to Western knowledge, but may have neglected traditional education; Environmental Degradation/Unsustainable resource use for colonial gain.

Chapter 8: The Struggle for Liberty: Independence Movements Across Africa

The winds of change swept across Africa in the 20th century. While the last chapter examined the complex nature of European colonization, this chapter portrays the inspiring stories of resistance and liberation. It is a new way of seeing the struggles, strategies, and triumphs that reshaped the political landscape of this continent.

The era of colonial rule did not extinguish the spirit of freedom that burned so brightly in African societies. People from all walks of life joined the struggle for self-determination – chefs, intellectuals, farmers, and workers. The chapter analyzes armed uprisings and non-violent protests, shows the leaders who dared to rise and inspire their people, and unveils the common ideals serving as a rallying point.

The chapter will show the different paths that African nations have taken toward independence. You can see the successes and failures of the independence movements in regions of diverse experiences across the continent.

Independence Movements in Africa

Such independence movements emerged across Africa from the 1960s on. They shattered European colonial rule and carved a whole new path for self-determination. This section tells outstanding accounts from the history of movements, bringing to the fore the leading figures behind them as well as the challenges faced on their way to freedom.

Resistance:

African resistance to colonialism was widely understood not as one but as *a series* of uprisings against oppression. Here, we take a glimpse at some of the common strategies used:

- **Armed Resistance:** In some situations, armed conflict against the colonial forces was the only viable option for Africans. In Algeria, Ahmed Ben Bella led a liberation war against the European power system, while in Angola, Agostinho Neto did likewise.

- **Non-violent Resistance:** Influenced by leaders like Mahatma Gandhi, strategies adopted particularly in Ghana, like those of Kwame Nkrumah, included non-violent protests, strikes, and boycotts targeting colonial powers.

- **Political Agitation:** Intellectuals and political leaders formed parties and organizations that sought self-rule. These groups made people aware, achieved mass mobilization, and lobbied within the international system.

- **Cultural Awakening:** The defense of traditional languages, religion, and customs was one of the strongest forms of resistance to cultural assimilation supported by various colonial regimes. In Senegal, leaders like Léopold Sédar Senghor advocated the importance of African cultural identity.

Challenges and Triumphs:

The road to independence was littered with obstacles. The major hindrances faced by such movements are outlined as follows:

- **Major Repression:** Colonial regimes often met resistance with brutality, attempting to squelch this dissension effectively through violence and imprisonment.

- **Division and Coercion:** Colonial powers used ethnic or regional divisions at times as a tactic to weaken resistance to their administration.

- **Economic Dependence:** Relying on colonial economies, some African countries operated under the threat of facing economic ruin if they sought independence.

Yet, irrespective of these challenges, the movements persisted. International support for decolonization was on the rise, and the moral voices clamoring for self-determination began to penetrate the conscience. At last, the cumulative force of resistance, international pressures, and changing world politics put an end to the colonial empires in Africa.

Heroes of the Struggle:

Dedication and relentless leadership lent shape to perhaps many more movements. Some legendary figures are presented below:

- **Kwame Nkrumah (Ghana):** A super charismatic leader who spearheaded Ghana's movement for independence and was the first president of the country.

- **Nelson Mandela (South Africa):** An anti-apartheid revolutionary imprisoned for 27 years who became the first black president of South Africa.

- **Jomo Kenyatta (Kenya):** Leader of the independence movement in Kenya who became the first president of Kenya.

- **Ahmed Ben Bella (Algeria):** Key leader of the Algerian War of Independence and the first president of independent Algeria.

- **Wangari Maathai (Kenya):** A well-received environmental and social justice activist, she tirelessly fought valiantly to raise her opinion on democracy and sustainable development in Kenya.

A Legacy of Inspiration:

The fight for the independence of African states stands as an invincible display of the possibilities contained within the human spirit – a strong will against the fundamental right of freedom. This is a story of bravery, sacrifice, and unwavering belief in a tomorrow of their own making. The struggles commemorate the contextual understanding of the ongoing challenges and opportunities framing African nations today.

Multiple Choice

Choose the answer that best completes each statement.

1. Who was the first President of Ghana, a key figure in the fight for African independence?

    A) Patrice Lumumba

    B) Julius Nyerere

    C) Kwame Nkrumah

2. The ideology that emphasized unity and cooperation among African nations is known as:

    A) Socialism

    B) Pan-Africanism

    C) Negritude

3. Which strategy involved non-violent protests and civil disobedience to pressure colonial authorities?

    A) Armed Uprising

    B) Cultural Revival

    C) Non-Violent Resistance

4. A famous leader of the anti-apartheid movement in South Africa was:

    A) Jomo Kenyatta

    B) Nelson Mandela

    C) Kwame Nkrumah

5. Which nation's independence movement was led by Ahmed Ben Bella?

    A) Ghana

    B) Kenya

    C) Algeria

6. The Mau Mau Uprising was a violent resistance movement against British rule in:

    A) Nigeria

    B) Kenya

    C) Angola

7. A common tactic employed by colonial powers to weaken resistance movements was to exploit:

A) Religious Differences

B) Educational Opportunities

C) Ethnic Divisions

8. Nnamdi Azikiwe was a prominent leader who co-founded a nationalist party advocating for independence in:

A) Ghana

B) Senegal

C) Nigeria

9. Which leader is associated with the concept of Negritude, celebrating African cultural heritage?

A) Kwame Nkrumah

B) Léopold Sédar Senghor

C) Jomo Kenyatta

10. The dismantling of European colonial empires in Africa is often referred to as:

A) Unification

B) Decolonization

C) Liberation

True or False

Distinguish fact from fiction with these statements about the fight for independence in Africa.

1. Africa saw a wave of independence movements in the mid-20th century, leading to the decolonization of many nations.

   o True

   o False

2. All African independence movements relied solely on armed struggle to achieve their goals.

   o True

   o False

3. Pan-Africanism is a philosophy that promotes conflict and competition between African nations.
   o True
   o False

4. Cultural revival efforts, emphasizing traditional languages and customs, were a key strategy for some independence movements.
   o True
   o False

5. European powers always granted independence peacefully when faced with strong resistance movements.
   o True
   o False

6. Jomo Kenyatta was a prominent leader in the fight for Kenyan independence.
   o True
   o False

7. Léopold Sédar Senghor is associated with advocating for the assimilation of African cultures into European ones.
   o True
   o False

8. Nnamdi Azikiwe co-founded a political party that campaigned for Nigerian independence.
   o True
   o False

9. The dismantling of apartheid in South Africa marked the end of all racial tensions in the country.
   o True
   o False

10. Understanding the era of African independence movements is irrelevant to comprehending contemporary Africa.
    o True
    o False

Fill in the Blank

Can you recall the key figures, places, and concepts related to African independence movements? Fill in the blank with the appropriate terms.

1. Nelson Mandela was the first Black President of _____ after the end of apartheid.

2. The ideology that emphasizes unity and cooperation among African nations is known as _____.

3. A famous leader of the anti-apartheid movement in South Africa was _____.

4. Which nation's independence movement was led by Ahmed Ben Bella? _____.

5. The Mau Mau Uprising was a violent resistance movement against British rule in _____.

6. A common tactic employed by colonial powers to weaken resistance movements was to exploit _____ divisions.

7. Nnamdi Azikiwe was a prominent leader who co-founded a nationalist party advocating for independence in _____.

8. Which leader is associated with the concept of Negritude, celebrating African cultural heritage? _____.

9. The dismantling of European colonial empires in Africa is often referred to as _____.

10. The philosophy that used to justify European dominance in Africa is known as _____.

One-Word Answer Questions

1. What general strategy did many independence movements use to achieve their goals?

   Response: _____.

2. What system of racial segregation did many African nations fight to overthrow?

   Response: _____.

3. What famous non-violent resistance leader fought against British rule in India? (Influenced many African leaders)

   Response: _____.

4. What country gained independence from France in 1960, led by Léopold Sédar Senghor?

   Response: _____.

5. Name the South African activist and Nobel laureate who campaigned against apartheid.

   Response: _____.

6. What natural resources did many European nations exploit in Africa during the colonial era?

   Response: _____.

7. What international organization played a role in advocating for decolonization?

   Response: _____.

8. What year did Ghana gain independence from Britain, becoming the first sub-Saharan African nation to do so?

   Response: _____.

9. Which South African liberation movement did Nelson Mandela lead?

   Response: _____.

10. What term describes the forced movement of Africans across the Atlantic Ocean during the slave trade?

    Response: _____.

Quick Fact Match

1. Match the important figures with their role in the anti-colonial movement.

   o Kwame Nkrumah ( ) Leader of the Algerian National Liberation Front (FLN)

   o Nelson Mandela ( ) First Prime Minister of Ghana after independence

   o Patrice Lumumba ( ) Imprisoned by the South African apartheid regime for 27 years

2. Match the African nation with its year of independence from colonial rule.

   o Kenya ( ) 1960

   o Angola ( ) 1975

   o Nigeria ( ) 1963

3. Match the colony with the European nation that colonized it.

   o Algeria ( ) Great Britain

   o Democratic Republic of the Congo (DRC) ( ) Belgium

   o Kenya ( ) France

4. Match the leader with their respective African nation or role in decolonization.

   o Jomo Kenyatta ( ) The first president of Kenya

   o Léopold Sédar Senghor ( ) Advocated for "Negritude," a celebration of black culture

   o Gamal Abdel Nasser ( ) Egyptian leader who overthrew the British-backed monarchy

5. Match the independence movement with its primary strategy.

   o Mau Mau Uprising ( ) Armed resistance against British rule in Kenya

   o Algerian War of Independence ( ) Guerilla warfare against French colonial forces

   o Kenyan African National Union (KANU) ( ) Political party that advocated for Kenyan independence through peaceful means

6. Match the pan-African leader with their ideology.
   o Marcus Garvey ( ) Pan-Africanism, unity of all people of African descent
   o Kwame Nkrumah ( ) Advocated for a return to Africa for the African diaspora (Back-to-Africa movement)
   o Nnamdi Azikiwe ( ) Believed in uniting the various ethnic groups in Nigeria

7. Match the effect of colonialism on Africa with an example.
   o Exploitation of resources ( ) The imposition of cash crop production for export over subsistence farming
   o Loss of traditional culture ( ) The suppression of Indigenous languages and religions
   o Artificial borders dividing ethnic groups ( ) The drawing of borders by European powers without regard to ethnic or cultural factors

8. Match the post-colonial challenge with an attempt to address it.
   o Authoritarian rule by newly independent leaders ( ) Formation of regional economic unions (e.g., ECOWAS)
   o Economic dependence on former colonial powers ( ) Democratization movements
   o Ethnic conflict and civil war ( ) Truth and Reconciliation commissions

9. Match the following anti-colonial revolts with the countries in which they took place:
   o Soweto Uprising ( ) Kenya
   o Angolan War of Independence ( ) South Africa
   o Mau Mau Uprising ( ) Angola

10. Match the ideology with its concept.
    o Pan-Africanism ( ) Unity and cooperation among African nations
    o Social Darwinism ( ) European dominance justified by "survival of the fittest"
    o Negritude ( ) Celebration of African cultural heritage

Answers

Multiple Choice Answers

1. **C) Kwame Nkrumah** (Kwame Nkrumah was a key figure in Ghana's fight for independence and became the country's first president.)

2. **B) Pan-Africanism** (Pan-Africanism is an ideology that emphasizes the unity and cooperation of African nations.)

3. **C) Non-Violent Resistance** (Non-violent resistance involves using tactics like protests and boycotts to achieve political goals.)

4. **B) Nelson Mandela** (Nelson Mandela was a prominent leader in the fight against apartheid in South Africa.)

5. **C) Algeria** (Ahmed Ben Bella was a key figure in Algeria's war for independence from France.)

6. **B) Kenya** (The Mau Mau Uprising was a violent struggle against British colonial rule in Kenya.)

7. **C) Ethnic Divisions** (Colonial powers sometimes exploited existing ethnic tensions to weaken resistance movements.)

8. **C) Nigeria** (Nnamdi Azikiwe co-founded the National Council of Nigeria and the Cameroons (NCNC), a party advocating for Nigerian independence.)

9. **B) Léopold Sédar Senghor** (Léopold Sédar Senghor was a leader in Senegal's independence movement and a proponent of Negritude, a concept celebrating African cultural heritage.)

10. **B) Decolonization** (Decolonization refers to the process of dismantling colonial empires and establishing independent nations.)

True or False Answers

1. **True** (Africa saw a surge of independence movements in the mid-20th century, leading to the decolonization of many European colonies.)

2. **False** (Many independence movements employed non-violent tactics like protests and boycotts alongside, or instead of, armed struggle.)

3. **False** (Pan-Africanism is an ideology that emphasizes unity, cooperation, and solidarity among African nations.)

4. **True** (Cultural revival was a strategy for some movements to strengthen national identity and resist the cultural assimilation policies of colonial powers.)

5. **False** (European powers often resorted to violence and repression to suppress independence movements.)

6. **True** (Jomo Kenyatta was a leading figure in Kenya's independence movement and became the country's first president.)

7. **False** (Léopold Sédar Senghor, a leader in Senegal's independence movement, is associated with the concept of Negritude, which celebrates African cultural heritage.)

8. **True** (Nnamdi Azikiwe co-founded the National Council of Nigeria and the Cameroons (NCNC), a party advocating for Nigerian independence.)

9. **False** (Dismantling apartheid was a crucial step, but racial issues persist in South Africa.)

10. **False** (Understanding the struggles for independence sheds light on the development challenges and opportunities faced by Africa today.)

Fill-in-the-Blank Answers

1. **South Africa** (Nelson Mandela became the first black president of South Africa after the dismantling of apartheid.)

2. **Pan-Africanism** (Pan-Africanism is an ideology that emphasizes unity and cooperation among African nations.)

3. **Nelson Mandela**

4. **Algeria** (Ahmed Ben Bella was a key figure in Algeria's war for independence from France.)

5. **Kenya** (The Mau Mau Uprising was a violent struggle against British colonial rule in Kenya.)

6. **Ethnic** (Colonial powers sometimes exploited existing ethnic tensions to weaken resistance movements.)

7. **Nigeria** (Nnamdi Azikiwe co-founded the National Council of Nigeria and the Cameroons (NCNC), a party advocating for Nigerian independence.)

8. **Léopold Sédar Senghor** (Léopold Sédar Senghor was a leader in Senegal's independence movement and a proponent of Negritude, a concept celebrating African cultural heritage.)

9. **Decolonization** (Decolonization refers to the process of dismantling colonial empires and establishing independent nations.)

10. **Social Darwinism** (Social Darwinism was a philosophy that used ideas of "survival of the fittest" to justify European dominance in Africa.)

One-Word Answers

1. Guerilla Warfare, Resistance (Many independence movements used tactics like surprise attacks and civil disobedience.)

2. Apartheid (South Africa's system of racial segregation.)

3. Gandhi (Mohandas Gandhi)

4. Senegal

5. Mandela (Nelson Mandela)

6. Minerals (Gold, diamonds, etc.)

7. United Nations (UN)

8. 1957

9. ANC (African National Congress)

10. Transatlantic Slave Trade

Quick Fact Match Answers

1. Kwame Nkrumah/First Prime Minister of Ghana after independence; Nelson Mandela/Imprisoned by the South African apartheid regime for 27 years; Patrice Lumumba/Leader of the Democratic Republic of the Congo (DRC) independence movement, assassinated shortly after independence.

2. Kenya/1963; Angola/1975; Nigeria/1960.

3. Algeria/France; Democratic Republic of the Congo (DRC)/Belgium; Kenya/Great Britain.

4. Jomo Kenyatta/First president of Kenya; Léopold Sédar Senghor/Advocated for "Negritude," a celebration of black culture; Gamal Abdel Nasser/Egyptian leader who overthrew the British-backed monarchy.

5. Mau Mau Uprising/Armed resistance against British rule in Kenya; Algerian War of Independence/Guerilla warfare against French colonial forces; Kenyan African National Union (KANU)/Political party that advocated for Kenyan independence through peaceful means.

6. Marcus Garvey/Advocated for a return to Africa for the African diaspora (Back-to-Africa movement); Kwame Nkrumah/Pan-Africanism, unity of all people of African descent; Nnamdi Azikiwe/Believed in uniting the various ethnic groups in Nigeria.

7. The exploitation of resources/The imposition of cash crop production for export over subsistence farming; Loss of traditional culture/The suppression of Indigenous languages and religions; Artificial borders dividing ethnic groups/The drawing of borders by European powers without regard to ethnic or cultural factors.

8. Authoritarian rule by newly independent leaders/Democratization movements; Economic dependence on former colonial powers/Formation of regional economic unions (e.g., ECOWAS); Ethnic conflict and civil war/Truth and Reconciliation commissions.

9. Soweto Uprising/South Africa; Angolan War of Independence/Angola; Mau Mau Uprising/Kenya.

10. Pan-Africanism/Unity and cooperation among African nations; Social Darwinism/European dominance justified by "survival of the fittest"; Negritude/Celebration of African cultural heritage.

Chapter 9: Modern Marvels: Africa's Rising Cities and Technologies

Having explored the powerful stories of independence struggles, we now turn our attention to an Africa that is dynamic, evolving, and full of promise. This chapter unveils the essence of a continent on the rise – one that defies outdated stereotypes of poverty and despair.

Modern Africa is home to expanding metropolises, cutting-edge technological advancements, and vibrant, thriving cultures. Once-quiet towns have transformed into economic powerhouses, with cities like Lagos and Nairobi boasting impressive skylines punctuated by skyscrapers. At the same time, innovative tech hubs are driving groundbreaking developments.

This chapter delves into the key forces behind Africa's urban renaissance, the rapid economic growth reshaping the continent, and the technological innovations propelling it into the future.

Modern Africa

Africa is a continent rich in diversity. From its growing megacities to ancient cultures, this very varied continent is home to no fewer than 2,000 languages and a whole lot of traditions. This vibrancy extends towards its rapidly growing economies as a central place of innovation.

- **Rising Urbanization:** Cities in Africa burst alive. This could mean either an opportunity or a challenge. Modern infrastructure projects create new economic hubs, coupled with the promise of a new, youthful generation of tech-savvy persons.

- **Fast Technologies and Connectivity:** Africa is speeding up big time with technology." Mobile money platforms redefine total financial inclusion. Home-grown tech startups are solving local issues from fresh perspectives.

- **An Emerging Powerhouse:** Quite resourceful and with a hugely attractive youthful citizenry. Several African nations are moving away from reliance on donor aid to sustainable development and emphasizing self-sufficient economic development.

- **A Global Player:** Africa has stopped sitting on the sidelines of the world stage. Its countries are increasingly taking leadership roles within their international organizations while creating strong partnerships with other nations around the world.

The saga of modern-day Africa continues with progress and promise. While challenges are here and don't shy away, Africa's invincible spirit and its inherent ability to innovate promise a shiny future.

Innovations and Achievements in Modern Africa

Africa is bursting with innovation and achievement. From tackling global challenges with local ingenuity to showcasing artistic brilliance on the world stage, the continent is making its mark.

Tech Savvy Solutions:

- **Medical Marvels:** The Cardio Pad is an electronic device invented by a Cameroonian doctor, Arthur Zang, for remote diagnosis of heart ailments. It has provided the key solution to solving important health problems through this affordable device.

- **Rat Power:** The organization uses giant African pouched rats to search for landmines and human tuberculosis in the training facilities in Tanzania – a cheap yet lifesaving approach.

- **Digital Innovations:** The digital laser developed by South African scientist Sandile Ngcobo is the first in the world to produce a genuine beam of light, opening up limitless possibilities in various industries.

Cultural Powerhouse:

- **Fashion Forward:** African designers have taken the world by storm. Colorful prints and bold silhouettes redefine and lead global fashion trends.

- **Literary Luminaries:** Africa makes its voice heard through authors like Chimamanda Ngozi Adichie and Ngũgĩ wa Thiong'o whose multi-layered narratives and vision are engaging enthusiasts globally.

- **Musical Mastery:** From the sweet sounds of Afrobeats to the flowing melodies of Highlife, African music has continued to electrify its audiences all over. Icons like Burna Boy and Yemi Alade have put African sounds in the spotlight.

These are just a few examples of the many ways Africa is innovating and achieving. The continent's rich cultural heritage and problem-solving spirit ensure that Africa's story is one of progress and inspiration.

Multiple Choice

1. Which African city is known as the "Silicon Savannah" due to its growing tech industry?

   A) Nairobi

   B) Cairo

   C) Johannesburg

2. What organization trains African giant pouched rats for lifesaving tasks like detecting landmines?

   A) Doctors Without Borders

   B) APOPO

   C) International Red Cross

3. Dr. Arthur Zang, a medical innovator from which African country, created the Cardio Pad for heart disease diagnosis?

   A) Nigeria

   B) South Africa

   C) Cameroon

4. What is the name of the groundbreaking digital laser invented by Sandile Ngcobo, a South African scientist?
   A) Afrolaser
   B) Madikwe Laser
   C) Digital Laser

5. Chimamanda Ngozi Adichie, a celebrated author, hails from which African nation?
   A) Kenya
   B) Nigeria
   C) Ghana

6. Afrobeats, a popular music genre with global recognition, has its roots in which part of Africa?
   A) West Africa
   B) East Africa
   C) Southern Africa

7. What is the term used to describe the rapid development of technological hubs in some African cities?
   A) Digital Oasis
   B) Silicon Savannah
   C) Tech Jungle

8. Besides Nairobi, which other city is a strong contender for being a major African tech hub?
   A) Lagos, Nigeria
   B) Cape Town, South Africa
   C) Addis Ababa, Ethiopia

9. What are some of the challenges faced by African cities as they strive for technological advancement?
   A) Lack of skilled workforce and infrastructure
   B) Limited access to funding and investment
   C) Both A & B

10. How can innovation and technological progress benefit Africa's development?
   A) Improved healthcare, education, and economic opportunities
   B) Increased global competitiveness and job creation
   C) Both A & B

True or False

Can you split the facts from false information?

1. Africa is the world's second-most populous continent.
    - o True
    - o False

2. Most of Africa's population lives in rural areas.
    - o True
    - o False

3. The use of mobile phones and mobile banking is rapidly growing in Africa.
    - o True
    - o False

4. Africa has very little technological innovation due to a lack of resources.
    - o True
    - o False

5. Kigali, Rwanda, is known for its car-free zones and focus on sustainability.
    - o True
    - o False

6. There are very few tech startups and innovation hubs in Africa.
    - o True
    - o False

7. Africa is experiencing a brain drain, with many skilled professionals leaving the continent.
    - o True
    - o False

8. Cape Town, South Africa, is a leader in developing solutions for renewable energy.
    - o True
    - o False

9. M-Pesa, a mobile money transfer service, originated in Europe.
   o True
   o False

10. Sanitation and access to clean water are major challenges facing most African cities.
    o True
    o False

Fill in the Blank

Fill in the blank with the word or phrase that best completes the statement.

1. Africa is the world's second-most populous continent, after _____.

2. The rapid growth of cities in Africa is known as _____.

3. _____ is a mobile money transfer service that has revolutionized financial inclusion in Africa.

4. Kigali, Rwanda, is a leader in developing _____ cities.

5. Many African countries are creating _____ hubs to foster technological innovation.

6. A major challenge facing African cities is the lack of access to _____.

7. Skilled professionals returning to Africa to contribute their expertise is called _____.

8. Cape Town, South Africa, is a center for research in _____ energy.

9. _____ is a popular Nigerian musician known for his Afrobeat music and activism.

10. _____ refers to the transfer of skilled labor out of a country.

One-Word Answer Questions

1. Name the Ethiopian capital, which hosts the African Union headquarters.

   Response: _____.

2. Lagos, Nigeria, is the most populous city in Africa. True or False?

   Response: _____.

3. What continent is leading the world in mobile phone money transfer services?

   Response: _____.

4. Kibera, located near Nairobi, is the largest informal settlement in Africa. True or False?

   Response: _____.

5. What resource is putting immense strain on some of Africa's growing cities?

   Response: _____.

6. One of the fastest-growing economies in the world is located in East Africa. What country is it?

   Response: _____.

7. Name the megalopolis stretching from Lagos to Abidjan.

   Response: _____.

8. What vast desert is being transformed by solar energy projects?

   Response: _____.

9. M-Pesa is a mobile money transfer service that originated in which East African country?

   Response: _____.

10. What natural resource is a major source of revenue for many African countries?

    Response: _____.

Quick Fact Match

Match the following innovations and organizations with their descriptions. Write the letter in the blank.

1. **Match the innovation with its impact on modern Africa.**
   - o   M-Pesa mobile banking ( ) Amplified traditional entertainment
   - o   Nollywood film industry ( ) Promotes continental unity and cooperation
   - o   African Union ( ) Digitized economy

2. **Match the technological advancement with its description.**
   - o   Silicon Savannah ( ) Genre combining African rhythms with funk and jazz
   - o   Afrobeat music ( ) Technology applied to improve agriculture
   - o   Agritech ( ) Nickname for Kenya's tech hub

3. **Match the fashion movement with its focus.**
   - o   Batik dyeing ( ) Modern take on traditional West African clothing
   - o   Ankara prints ( ) Traditional resist-dyeing technique using wax
   - o   Snwali fashion ( ) Boldly-colored fabrics with vibrant patterns

4. **Match the landmark with the city where it's found.**
   - o   The Palace of the Sultan of Morocco ( ) Johannesburg
   - o   The Great Mosque of Djenné ( ) Djenné
   - o   The Nelson Mandela Centre of Memory ( ) Marrakech

5. **Match the literary award with the continent on which it focuses.**
   - o   Man Booker Prize ( ) Recognizes excellence in African literature written in English
   - o   Caine Prize for African Writing ( ) Awarded to authors of any nationality
   - o   Nobel Prize in Literature ( ) Focuses on works published in the UK and the Commonwealth

6. Match the artist with their artistic expression.
   - Chimamanda Ngozi Adichie ( ) Powerful Asante warrior queen
   - Yaa Asantewaa ( ) Fictional superhero film celebrating African culture
   - Black Panther ( ) Award-winning novelist

7. Match the environmental initiative with its goal.
   - The Great Green Wall ( ) Transforms plastic waste into valuable products
   - Kibera Plastic Recycling Project ( ) Promotes eco-friendly clothing production
   - Sustainable fashion movement ( ) Massive tree-planting project to combat desertification

8. Match the economic term with its definition.
   - Microfinance ( ) African Continental Free Trade Area
   - AfCFTA ( ) Small loans to support entrepreneurs
   - Social entrepreneurship ( ) Businesses that aim to solve social problems

9. Match the technological advancement with its application.
   - Drones ( ) Securing digital transactions
   - Virtual reality ( ) Delivering medical supplies to remote areas
   - Blockchain technology ( ) Showcasing historical landmarks for tourism

10. Match the educational program with its focus.
    - Ashesi University ( ) Specializes in science, technology, engineering, and mathematics (STEM) fields
    - University of Nairobi ( ) Develops future leaders across the continent
    - African Leadership Academy ( ) Offers a problem-solving, ethics-based curriculum

While you bring your exploration of the emerging cities and technologies in Africa to a close, there is a clear and insightful narrative. It represents something other than a land of old cultures and geographical beauty. It is a continent full of innovation, enthusiasm, and a clear will to self-actualize.

The developments you have seen, from mobile banking solutions to robust film industries, are not merely technological breakthroughs; they are agents of change that are altering economies and providing hope for the future. It is the oncoming wave of youth in Africa, a demographic explosion, that has moved to lead those changes. With their innovation, entrepreneurship, and focus on the common good, they are writing a new story for the continent.

Answers

Multiple Choice

1. **A) Nairobi** (Nairobi, the capital of Kenya, has earned the nickname "Silicon Savannah" due to its rapidly growing tech industry. The city is a hub for startups, innovation centers, and international tech companies.)

2. **B) APOPO** (APOPO, a non-profit organization headquartered in Tanzania, trains African giant pouched rats for various detection tasks. These intelligent rodents are particularly adept at sniffing out landmines and tuberculosis, saving lives in conflict zones and healthcare settings.)

3. **C) Cameroon** (Dr. Arthur Zang, a medical doctor and innovator from Cameroon, is the mind behind the Cardio Pad. This portable device makes diagnosing heart disease more accessible in remote areas with limited medical resources.)

4. **C) Digital Laser** (Sandile Ngcobo, a South African scientist, is credited with inventing the world's first functional digital laser, a significant advancement with potential applications in various fields such as telecommunications and medicine. The invention is referred to as the Digital Laser.)

5. **B) Nigeria** (Chimamanda Ngozi Adichie, a renowned author known for her powerful storytelling and social commentary, is originally from Nigeria.)

6. **A) West Africa** (Afrobeats, an energetic music genre characterized by its complex rhythms and often incorporating elements of electronic music, originated in West Africa.)

7. **B) Silicon Savannah** (The term "Silicon Savannah" is a play on "Silicon Valley" in the United States and refers to the emerging tech hubs springing up in various African cities, like Nairobi, Lagos, and Cape Town.)

8. **A) Lagos, Nigeria** (Lagos, the economic powerhouse of Nigeria, is another major contender for the title of Africa's leading tech hub. The city boasts a thriving startup scene and is attracting significant investment in the tech sector.)

9. **C) Both A & B** (African cities face a multitude of challenges in their pursuit of technological advancement. Lack of skilled professionals and inadequate infrastructure are significant hurdles. Additionally, limited access to funding and investment can hamper the growth of innovative startups and businesses.)

10. **C) Both A & B** (Innovation and technological progress hold immense potential for Africa's development. These advancements can lead to improvements in healthcare, education, and economic opportunities across the continent. Furthermore, Africa's growing tech sector can boost its global competitiveness and create new job markets.)

True or False

1. **True** (Africa is the world's second-most populous continent, after Asia.)

2. **False** (While Africa still has a significant rural population, urbanization is happening rapidly in many countries.)

3. **True** (Mobile phone usage and mobile banking solutions like M-Pesa are transforming financial inclusion across Africa.)

4. **False** (Africa has a growing tech sector with innovative solutions being developed for local challenges.)

5. **True** (Kigali is a pioneering city focusing on green initiatives and sustainable urban development.)

6. **False** (Tech startups and innovation hubs are flourishing in many African countries.)

7. **False** (While there is some brain drain, there's also a growing trend of skilled professionals returning to Africa.)

8. **True** (Cape Town is a hub for renewable energy research and development.)

9. **False** (M-Pesa, a highly successful mobile money transfer service, was launched in Kenya.)

10. **True** (Lack of proper sanitation and access to clean water are critical issues that many African cities are working to address.)

Fill-in-the-Blank Answers

1. **Asia** (Africa is the world's second-largest inhabited continent by population.)

2. **Urbanization** (The rapid increase in the number of people living in cities.)

3. **M-Pesa** (A Kenyan mobile phone-based money transfer service.)

4. **Sustainable** (Focusing on environmentally friendly practices and long-term development.)

5. **Innovation** (Spaces where new ideas and technologies are developed.)

6. **Clean water** (Many African cities struggle to provide clean water to all residents.)

7. **Reverse brain drain** (The trend of skilled professionals returning to their home countries.)

8. **Renewable** (Energy sources that can be replenished naturally.)

9. **Fela Kuti** (The pioneer of Afrobeat music and a famous Nigerian activist.)

10. **Brain drain** (The emigration of skilled workers from a country.)

One-Word Answers

1. **Addis Ababa** (Addis Ababa is the capital of Ethiopia and the headquarters of the African Union.)

2. **True** (Lagos, Nigeria is the most populous city in Africa, with a population exceeding 20 million.)

3. **Africa** (Africa is leading the world in mobile phone money transfer services, with services like M-Pesa playing a vital role in financial inclusion.)

4. **True** (Kibera, located near Nairobi, Kenya, is considered the largest informal settlement in Africa.)

5. **Water** (Water scarcity is a major challenge for some of Africa's rapidly growing cities, straining infrastructure and resources.)

6. **Ethiopia** (Ethiopia is one of the fastest-growing economies in the world, with a focus on infrastructure development and technological advancements.)

7. **Lagos-Abidjan megalopolis** (This developing megalopolis stretches along the West African coast, encompassing major cities in several countries.)

8. **Sahara Desert** (Large-scale solar energy projects are being developed in the Sahara Desert, harnessing its vast potential for renewable energy.)

9. **Kenya** (M-Pesa, a pioneering mobile money transfer service, originated in Kenya and has revolutionized financial transactions across Africa.)

10. **Minerals** (Minerals like cobalt, coltan, and diamonds are a major source of revenue for many African countries, though ethical sourcing remains a concern.)

Quick Fact Match Answers

1. M-Pesa mobile banking/Digitized economy; Nollywood film industry/Amplified traditional entertainment; African Union/Promotes continental unity and cooperation.

2. Silicon Savannah/Nickname for Kenya's tech hub; Afrobeat music/Genre combining African rhythms with funk and jazz; Agritech/Technology applied to improve agriculture.

3. Batik dyeing/Traditional resist-dyeing technique using wax; Ankara prints/Boldly-colored fabrics with vibrant patterns; Snwali fashion/Modern take on traditional West African clothing.

4. The Palace of the Sultan of Morocco/Marrakech; The Great Mosque of Djenné/Djenné; The Nelson Mandela Centre of Memory/Johannesburg.

5. Man Booker Prize/Focuses on works published in the UK and the Commonwealth; Caine Prize for African Writing/Recognizes excellence in African literature written in English; Nobel Prize in Literature/Awarded to authors of any nationality.

6. Chimamanda Ngozi Adichie/Award-winning novelist; Yaa Asantewaa/Powerful Asante warrior queen; Black Panther/Fictional superhero film celebrating African culture.

7. The Great Green Wall/Massive tree-planting project to combat desertification; the Kibera Plastic Recycling Project/Transforms plastic waste into valuable products; Sustainable fashion movement/Promotes eco-friendly clothing production.

8. Microfinance/Small loans to support entrepreneurs; AfCFTA/African Continental Free Trade Area; Social entrepreneurship/Businesses that aim to solve social problems.

9. Drones/Delivering medical supplies to remote areas; Virtual reality/Showcasing historical landmarks for tourism; Blockchain technology/Securing digital transactions.

10. Ashesi University/Offers a problem-solving, ethics-based curriculum; the University of Nairobi/Specializes in science, technology, engineering, and mathematics (STEM) fields; African Leadership Academy/Develops future leaders across the continent.

Chapter 10: Voices of the Continent: Influential Africans in History and Today

Throughout history, Africa has had its fair share of great personalities who have turned the fortunes of the continent and affected the whole world. From the dauntless warriors who rose to face oppression to pliant visionary leaders who guided independence movements, and from the refreshing direction of artists who reinvented cultural expression to brilliant scientific minds famished to push the frontiers of Knowledge, great African culture can boast innumerable those who left an indelible mark.

This final chapter reveals the lists of some of these influential figures. However, instead of adopting a traditional narrative form, a brazen trivia journey would be undertaken. So, be ready for the quiz and get inspired by the great achievements of these iconic Africans.

Welcome, game changers, innovators, and cultural giants of Africa! The first question is here.

Inspirational African Figures

Africa's rich history and promising present are filled with remarkable individuals who have made lasting impacts in various fields. It's time to meet a few of these inspiring figures.

History Makers:

- **Mansa Musa (1312-1337):** The king of the West African empire of Mali, Mansa Musa was foremost a very wealthy monarch and a great patron of the arts and sciences. His notorious pilgrimage to Mecca, during which he famously distributed tremendous amounts of gold, secured for him a preeminently high place among the wealthiest people in history.

- **Yaa Asantewaa (1840-1921):** A fearless warrior queen of the Asante people of Ghana, Yaa Asantewaa fought deeply in resisting British incursions and rule. She rallied her troops and led them into battle, becoming a symbol of African resistance to European domination.

- **Wangari Maathai (1940-2011):** Wangari Maathai was a Kenyan environmentalist and a Nobel Peace Prize winner who organized the Green Belt Movement and planted millions of trees all over Africa. She was an activist for the environment and women and inspired a generation.

Contemporary Changemakers:

- **Mo Ibrahim (1946-Present):** A Sudanese-British billionaire and philanthropist, Mo Ibrahim is the founder of the Mo Ibrahim Foundation, which awards a prize to an African leader for good governance and stepping down after completion of one full term. He champions good governance and leadership across the continent.

- **Elon Musk (1971-Present):** Born and raised in South Africa, coupled with his vision, Elon Musk revolutionizes the tech realm and the space industry with companies like Tesla and SpaceX. While other business endeavors might find him off African shores, his African legacy still spurs young Africans to be ever-innovative and entreprencurial.

- **Chimamanda Ngozi Adichie (1977- Present):** Nigerian author Chimamanda Ngozi Adichie has captivated readers all over the world with her powerful stories that examine race, gender, and identity. She has become a powerful voice in contemporary literature, contesting stereotypes and celebrating narratives about Africa.

- **Caster Semenya (1991-Present):** A South African middle-distance runner who has been known for her incredible speed and perseverance, Semenya is a two-time Olympic champion. Though her adaptation to the life-changing ordeal with high testosterone levels posed challenges, she indeed remains an inspiration to women in sports and a beacon of hope consigned to challenging to break barriers.

These are just a few examples of the influential Africans who have shaped – and continue to shape – the continent and the world. With each new generation, fresh voices and remarkable achievements emerge. Keep exploring and learning about the extraordinary men and women who make Africa a beacon of innovation, resilience, and hope.

African Creativity and Cultural Expressions

Creatively coming out in almost all areas of life, Africa is a continent with a lot of artistic energy. The stylistic expressions of African music, literature, fashion, and arts are as diversified as the continent itself. Here are some of the fabulous forms of artistic expression, along with some of the most acclaimed artists who have carried them across the globe.

- **Music:** It is common knowledge that Africa is soul music up to the core. From the pulsating Afrobeat emanating from Nigeria, brought into the world by Fela Kuti, through the soulful mbalax made popular by Youssou N'Dour, African music continues to captivate audiences worldwide. Many modern artists today, like Angelique Kidjo and Burna Boy, are pushing the limits by blending traditional sounds with modern influences.

- **Literature:** Africa boasts probably one of the richest kinds of literature. Storytellers weave their tales in an eloquence that understands the cultural significance. Each of these illustrious authors, such as Chinua Achebe, whose novel "Things Fall Apart" elicited reactions to the shattering aftermath of colonialism, and Chimamanda Ngozi Adichie, whose compelling tales proffer insight into contemporary African experiences, has gained worldwide recognition. The African writer is still assailing stereotypes, offering them an undesigning eye on how the world is.

- **Art:** African art is a cornucopia of visual delights in varying styles and mediums; from the evocative and intricate bronze sculptures from the mystical court of the Kingdom of Benin to the vividly painted masks still used for initiation rites and other traditional ceremonies, African art laps with symbolism and cultural indices. Contemporary artists such as El Anatsui, who deconstructs and reassembles everyday materials, and Marlene Dumas, whose poignant paintings delve well into the realms of identity and race, are outrunners in the artistic race.

- **Fashion:** African fashion is a cocktail of tradition mixed with a good dose of modernity. Vivid colors, stunning in their patterns, and fabrics from local sources mark the distinctive character. Designers like Stella Jean, who mixes African and European influences, and Maki Oh, whose designs have been worn by Michelle Obama and Beyoncé, bring African fashion to the world stage.

This is just a glimpse into the vast and ever-growing world of African cultural expressions. Every region of Africa holds unique artistic traditions waiting to be explored. As you engage with Africa's heritage, let yourself be captivated by the beauty, richness, and vibrancy of the African spirit.

Multiple Choice

This section tests your knowledge about some of the most influential figures in African history and contemporary life. Choose the best answer for each question.

1. Who is the Nobel laureate known for her work advocating for girls' education in Africa?

   A) Chimamanda Ngozi Adichie

   B) Wangari Maathai

   C) Malala Yousafzai

2. Mansa Musa, a wealthy ruler in West Africa, was known for his patronage of what?

   A) Military expansion

   B) Arts and Sciences

   C) Religious conversion

3. A fearless warrior queen who resisted British colonialism in Ghana was:

   A) Winnie Mandela

   B) Yaa Asantewaa

   C) Ellen Johnson Sirleaf

4. The Mo Ibrahim Foundation awards a prize to recognize what kind of leadership in Africa?

   A) Economic growth

   B) Democratic governance

   C) Technological innovation

5. The environmental activist who founded the Green Belt Movement, credited with planting millions of trees across Africa, was:

   A) Wangari Maathai

   B) Chimamanda Ngozi Adichie

   C) Caster Semenya

6. A renowned Nigerian novelist known for her powerful stories exploring themes of race, gender, and identity is:

A) Chimamanda Ngozi Adichie

B) Winnie Mandela

C) Ngozi Okonjo-Iweala

7. A South African middle-distance runner and two-time Olympic gold medalist known for her perseverance is:

A) Caster Semenya

B) Angelique Kidjo

C) Winnie Mandela

8. A visionary entrepreneur who revolutionized the tech and space industries with companies like Tesla and SpaceX is:

A) Elon Musk

B) Mo Ibrahim

C) Akin Adesina

9. A prominent figure in Senegalese music known for popularizing the mbalax genre is:

A) Fela Kuti

B) Youssou N'Dour

C) Angelique Kidjo

10. A contemporary musician who has become a global icon, fusing traditional African sounds with modern influences, is:

A) Fela Kuti

B) Angelique Kidjo

C) Youssou N'Dour

True or False

Read each statement carefully and decide whether it is true or false.

1. African literature has gained international recognition with authors like Chinua Achebe and Ngũgĩ wa Thiong'o.
   o True
   o False

2. Mansa Musa, a wealthy ruler in West Africa, is credited with building the Great Wall of China.
   o True
   o False

3. Wangari Maathai, a Nobel laureate, was a prominent leader in the fight against apartheid in South Africa.
   o True
   o False

4. Elon Musk, a visionary entrepreneur, was born and raised in the United States.
   o True
   o False

5. Yaa Asantewaa, a fearless warrior queen, successfully defended her kingdom against British colonization.
   o True
   o False

6. The Mo Ibrahim Foundation awards a prize to African musicians who have achieved international fame.
   o True
   o False

7. Chimamanda Ngozi Adichie, a celebrated Nigerian novelist, is known for her children's books.
   o True
   o False

8. Caster Semenya, a South African athlete, holds the world record in the high jump.
   o True
   o False

9. Youssou N'Dour, a prominent musician, is known for his work in reggae music.
   o True
   o False

10. The Green Belt Movement, founded by Wangari Maathai, focuses on planting trees across Africa to combat desertification.
   o True
   o False

Fill in the Blank

Can you remember the names of these influential Africans? Fill in the blank with the most appropriate answer.

1. _____ is a celebrated Nigerian author best known for his novel, "Things Fall Apart."

2. Mansa Musa, a wealthy king in West Africa, was famous for his pilgrimage to _____.

3. _____, a fearless warrior queen from Ghana, resisted British colonialism.

4. The Mo Ibrahim Foundation recognizes African leaders who have demonstrated _____ governance.

5. Environmental activist, _____, founded the Green Belt Movement, which has planted millions of trees across Africa.

6. _____ is a visionary entrepreneur who revolutionized industries with companies like Tesla and SpaceX.

7. Renowned novelist, _____, is known for her powerful stories exploring themes of race, gender, and identity.

8. South African middle-distance runner, _____, is a two-time Olympic gold medalist.

9. _____, a prominent musician from Senegal, popularized the mbalax genre.

10. Contemporary musician, _____, has become a global icon, fusing traditional African sounds with modern influences.

One-Word Answer Questions

Can you identify these influential Africans with just one word?

1. Name the South African anti-apartheid revolutionary and former president.

   Response: _____.

2. What was the pilgrimage undertaken by Mansa Musa, king of the West African empire of Mali?

   Response: _____.

3. What term describes the racial segregation system dismantled in South Africa?

   Response: _____.

4. What is the name of the prize awarded by the Mo Ibrahim Foundation for democratic leadership in Africa?

   Response: _____.

5. What is the environmental challenge addressed by the Green Belt Movement?

   Response: _____.

6. What scientific field is Elon Musk's SpaceX company focused on?

   Response: _____.

7. Briefly describe the literary genre that Chimamanda Ngozi Adichie's novels are known for.

   Response: _____.

8. What is the name of the athletic event Caster Semenya competes in?

   Response: _____.

9. What musical genre did Youssou N'Dour popularize in Senegal?

   Response: _____.

10. How does Angelique Kidjo's music blend different influences?

    Response: _____.

Quick Fact Match

Match the following influential Africans with their descriptions. Write the letter in the blank.

1. Match the African artists with their respective fields of achievement.
   o Fela Kuti ( ) One of the world's leading contemporary artists
   o Lupita Nyong'o ( ) Award-winning actress known for her role in "12 Years a Slave"
   o El Anatsui ( ) Pioneer of Afrobeat music

2. Match the political leader with their country of leadership.
   o Nelson Mandela ( ) Liberia
   o Wangari Maathai ( ) South Africa
   o Ellen Johnson Sirleaf ( ) Kenya

3. Match the literary figure with their work.
   o Chinua Achebe ( ) Decolonizing the Mind
   o Chimamanda Ngozi Adichie ( ) "Things Fall Apart"
   o Ngũgĩ wa Thiong'o ( ) Americanah

4. Match the entrepreneur with their innovative company.
   o Mo Ibrahim ( ) Tesla
   o Akinwumi Adesina ( ) African Development Bank
   o Elon Musk ( ) Celtel

5. Match the athlete with their sport.
   o Caster Semenya ( ) Basketball
   o Didier Drogba ( ) Middle-distance running
   o Hakeem Olajuwon ( ) Football (Soccer)

6. Match the scientist with their area of expertise.
   o Francisca Nneke Okeke ( ) Trade Law
   o Amina Mohamed ( ) Supercomputing
   o Philip Emeagwali ( ) Astrofísica (Astrophysics)

7. Match the fashion designer with their signature style.
   o Stella Jean ( ) Streetwear with high-fashion elements
   o Maria Borges ( ) Fusion of African and European influences
   o Dapper Dan ( ) Advocates for body positivity and inclusivity

8. Match the filmmaker with their groundbreaking movie.
   o Abderrahmane Sissako ( ) Eve's Bayou
   o Kasi Lemmons ( ) Rafiki
   o Wanuri Kahiu ( ) Timbuktu

9. Match the musician with their instrument.
   o Salif Keita ( ) Vocals
   o Angelique Kidjo ( ) Flugelhorn (a trumpet variant)
   o Hugh Masekela ( ) Kora (a stringed instrument)

10. Match the architect with their innovative design.
    o David Adjaye ( ) Museum of Modern Art Africa (MOCAA)
    o Diébédo Francis Kéré ( ) Smithsonian National Museum of African American History and Culture
    o Mokena Makeka( ) Burkina Faso National Assembly

This chapter's stories offer a glimpse into the vast African talent and leadership. Every corner of the continent holds the promise of discoveries, including groundbreaking scientists, captivating artists, and passionate activists, all working to build a better Africa.

Through trivia questions and engaging facts, you've encountered various African changemakers, including warriors, artists, scientists, entrepreneurs, and leaders. Their achievements span centuries and touch upon every facet of human endeavor. From the unwavering courage of Yaa Asantewaa to the visionary innovation of Elon Musk, these remarkable individuals inspire people with their dedication, resilience, and unwavering belief in a brighter future.

Answers

Multiple Choice Answers

1. C) Malala Yousafzai (**Malala Yousafzai** is a Nobel laureate known for her work advocating for girls' education.)

2. B) Arts and Sciences (**Arts and sciences** was the field Mansa Musa was known for patronizing.)

3. B) Yaa Asantewaa (**Yaa Asantewaa** was the fearless warrior queen who resisted British colonialism in Ghana.)

4. B) Democratic governance (**Democratic governance** is what the Mo Ibrahim Foundation awards a prize for.)

5. A) Wangari Maathai (**Wangari Maathai** was the environmental activist who founded the Green Belt Movement.)

6. A) Chimamanda Ngozi Adichie (**Chimamanda Ngozi Adichie** is a renowned Nigerian novelist.)

7. A) Caster Semenya (**Caster Semenya** is a South African middle-distance runner and two-time Olympic gold medalist.)

8. A) Elon Musk (**Elon Musk** is the visionary entrepreneur who revolutionized the tech and space industries.)

9. B) Youssou N'Dour (**Youssou N'Dour** is a prominent figure in Senegalese music known for popularizing the mbalax genre.)

10. B) Angelique Kidjo (**Angelique Kidjo** is a contemporary musician who has become a global icon, fusing traditional African sounds with modern influences.)

True or False Answers

1. **True** (African literature has seen a surge in international recognition in recent decades.)

2. **False** (The Great Wall of China was built in East Asia, not West Africa.)

3. **False** (Apartheid was the racial segregation system in South Africa. Wangari Maathai was a Kenyan environmental activist.)

4. **False** (Elon Musk was born in South Africa.)

5. **False** (Yaa Asantewaa bravely resisted British colonialism, but her kingdom was eventually defeated.)

6. **False** (The Mo Ibrahim Foundation awards a prize to African leaders who have governed democratically.)

7. **False** (Chimamanda Ngozi Adichie is known for her novels that explore adult themes.)
8. **False** (Caster Semenya is a middle-distance runner, not a high jumper.)
9. **False** (Youssou N'Dour is known for popularizing the mbalax genre, a Senegalese style of music.)
10. **True** (The Green Belt Movement is a successful initiative that has addressed environmental challenges in Africa.)

Fill-in-the-Blank Answers

1. Chinua Achebe
2. Mecca
3. Yaa Asantewaa
4. Democratic
5. Wangari Maathai
6. Elon Musk
7. Chimamanda Ngozi Adichie
8. Caster Semenya
9. Youssou N'Dour
10. Angelique Kidjo

One-Word Answers

1. Mandela (Nelson Mandela)
2. Hajj
3. Apartheid
4. Governance (Good Governance)
5. Desertification
6. Space
7. Novels
8. Running
9. Mbalax
10. Traditional/Modern (Fusing traditional African sounds with modern influences)

Quick Fact Match Answers

1. Fela Kuti/Pioneer of Afrobeat music; Lupita Nyong'o/Award-winning actress known for her role in "12 Years a Slave"; El Anatsui/One of the world's leading contemporary artists.

2. Nelson Mandela/South Africa; Wangari Maathai/Kenya; Ellen Johnson Sirleaf/Liberia.

3. Chinua Achebe/Things Fall Apart; Chimamanda Ngozi Adichie/Americanah; Ngũgĩ wa Thiong'o/Decolonizing the Mind.

4. Mo Ibrahim/Celtel (founded Celtel, a mobile phone network operator); Akinwumi Adesina/African Development Bank (leads the African Development Bank); Elon Musk/Tesla (founded Tesla, an electric vehicle and clean energy company).

5. Caster Semenya/Middle-distance running; Didier Drogba/Football (Soccer); Hakeem Olajuwon/Basketball.

6. Francisca Nneka Okeke/Astrofísica (Astrophysics); Amina Mohamed/Trade Law; Philip Emeagwali/Supercomputing.

7. Stella Jean/Fusion of African and European influences; Maria Borges/Advocate for body positivity and inclusivity; Dapper Dan/Streetwear with high-fashion elements.

8. Abderrahmane Sissako/Timbuktu; Kasi Lemmons/Eve's Bayou; Wanuri Kahiu/Rafiki.

9. Salif Keita/Kora (a stringed instrument); Angelique Kidjo/Vocals; Hugh Masekela/Flugelhorn (a trumpet variant).

10. David Adjaye/Smithsonian National Museum of African American History and Culture; Diébédo Francis Kéré/Burkina Faso National Assembly; Mokena Makeka/Museum of Modern Art Africa (MOCAA).

Conclusion

You've made it to the finish line of your African history trivia adventure—congratulations! Take a moment to celebrate this victory of brainpower, perhaps with a refreshing glass of hibiscus tea, and bask in your newfound knowledge. But remember, trivia isn't just about keeping score or proving you're the sharpest mind in the room. It's about unlocking doors to fascinating subjects—like African history—and transforming a list of dry facts into an engaging and vibrant exploration.

This book is more than just a collection of questions and answers—it's a gateway to deeper discovery. Did a particular question spark your curiosity about an ancient kingdom, a revolutionary leader, or a groundbreaking innovation? Perfect! Let this be your launchpad. From here, dive into the rich, multilayered world of African history. There are countless books, documentaries, and online resources waiting to be explored, each revealing new layers of this vast and complex narrative.

The more you learn about Africa, the better you understand the world. Too often, Africa is reduced to clichés of jungles and safaris, but its story is far more intricate. Its past is woven with the rise and fall of mighty empires, groundbreaking innovations, and a resilience that continues to shape its present and future. Exploring its history unveils a continent teeming with diverse cultures, languages, and traditions, making it one of the most exciting places to study.

Africa's history is an ongoing saga, with new archaeological discoveries emerging every year, shedding fresh light on ancient civilizations and their achievements. This trivia book is just the beginning of your journey. Let the stories you've uncovered here fuel your curiosity and inspire you to keep exploring—not just Africa's past, but the wider world beyond.

If you enjoyed this book, a review on Amazon would be greatly appreciated because it would mean a lot to hear from you.

To leave a review:

1. Open your camera app.
2. Point your mobile device at the QR code.
3. The review page will appear in your web browser.

Thanks for your support!

Check out another book in the series

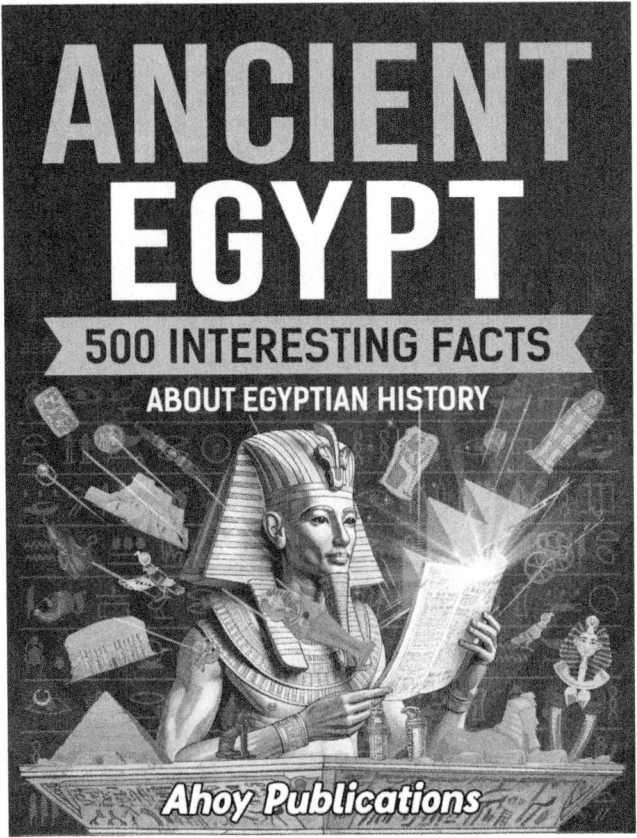

ANCIENT EGYPT
500 INTERESTING FACTS
ABOUT EGYPTIAN HISTORY
Ahoy Publications

Welcome Aboard, Check Out This Limited-Time Free Bonus!

Ahoy, reader! Welcome to the Ahoy Publications family, and thanks for snagging a copy of this book! Since you've chosen to join us on this journey, we'd like to offer you something special.

Check out the link below for a **FREE** e-book filled with delightful facts about American History.

But that's not all - you'll also have access to our exclusive email list with even more free e-books and insider knowledge. Well, what are ye waiting for? Click the link below to join and set sail toward exciting adventures in American History.

Access your bonus here

https://ahoypublications.com/

Or, Scan the QR code!

References

African Budget Safaris. (2019, September 3). African Budget Safaris. African Budget Safaris. https://www.africanbudgetsafaris.com/blog/african-tribes-african-culture-and-african-traditions/

Ancient Egypt. (2018, August 21). HISTORY. https://www.history.com/topics/ancient-egypt

Andrews, E. (2018, August 23). 7 Influential African Empires. HISTORY. https://www.history.com/news/7-influential-african-empires

Jarus, O. (2016, July 28). Ancient Egypt: A Brief History. Live Science; Live Science. https://www.livescience.com/55578-egyptian-civilization.html

Lincoln County Schools. (n.d.). Effects of Imperialism in Africa. https://www.lcsnc.org/cms/lib/NC01911169/Centricity/Domain/1414/Effects%20of%20Imperialism%20in%20Africa.pdf

National Geographic. (2023). Ancient Egypt | National Geographic Society. Education.nationalgeographic.org; National Geographic. https://education.nationalgeographic.org/resource/resource-library-ancient-egypt/

Office of the Historian. (2019). Decolonization of Asia and Africa, 1945–1960. State.gov. https://history.state.gov/milestones/1945-1952/asia-and-africa

Metcalfe, T. (2023, December 5). 7 extraordinary African kingdoms from ancient times to centuries ago. Livescience.com. https://www.livescience.com/archaeology/extraordinary-african-kingdoms-from-ancient-times-to-centuries-ago

The Story of Africa| BBC World Service. (n.d.). Www.bbc.co.uk. https://www.bbc.co.uk/worldservice/africa/features/storyofafrica/index_section3.shtml

Image References

1   https://www.publicdomainpictures.net/en/free-download.php?image=africa-map-vintage-art&id=413752

2   https://www.pexels.com/photo/reliefs-on-the-walls-of-an-ancient-egyptian-temple-in-luxor-18991553/

3   mharrsch, Attribution 2.0 Generic, CC BY 2.0 <https://creativecommons.org/licenses/by/2.0/deed.en > https://www.flickr.com/photos/mharrsch/19308840841

4   Mark Fischer, Attribution-ShareAlike 2.0 Generic, CC BY-SA 2.0, <https://creativecommons.org/licenses/by-sa/2.0/deed.en> https://www.flickr.com/photos/fischerfotos/23785641449

5   https://pixabay.com/id/illustrations/cleopatra-clipart-transparan-mesir-8938958/

6   British Museum, CC BY-SA 2.0 FR <https://creativecommons.org/licenses/by-sa/2.0/fr/deed.en>, via Wikimedia Commons. https://commons.wikimedia.org/wiki/File:Ramses_II-IMG_4382-black.jpg

7   Jon Bodsworth, Copyrighted free use, via Wikimedia Commons: https://commons.wikimedia.org/wiki/File:01_khafre_north.jpg

8   Walters Art Museum, Pulıc domain, via Wikimedia Commons: https://commons.wikimedia.org/wiki/File:Egyptian_-_Scarab_of_Hatshepsut_-_Walters_4260_-_Top.jpg

9   Yair Haklai, CC BY-SA 4.0 <https://creativecommons.org/licenses/by-sa/4.0>, via Wikimedia Commons: https://commons.wikimedia.org/wiki/File:Egyptian_mummies_in_%C3%84gyptisches_Museum_Berlin-2.jpg

10 Gary Todd from Xinzheng, China, CC0, via Wikimedia Commons: https://commons.wikimedia.org/wiki/File:Ancient_Egypt_Papyrus_Scroll_of_the_Dead_(28748821475).jpg

11 Avrand6, CC BY-SA 4.0 <https://creativecommons.org/licenses/by-sa/4.0>, via Wikimedia Commons: https://commons.wikimedia.org/wiki/File:Ushabti,_Denver_Museum_of_Nature_and_Science.jpg

12 en:User: Hajor, CC BY-SA 1.0 <https://creativecommons.org/licenses/by-sa/1.0>, via Wikimedia Commons: https://commons.wikimedia.org/wiki/File:Egypt.Giza.Sphinx.01.jpg

13 Jl FilpoC, CC BY-SA 4.0 <https://creativecommons.org/licenses/by-sa/4.0>, via Wikimedia Commons: https://commons.wikimedia.org/wiki/File:Amuleto_Ankh,_reinado_de_Tutankam%C3%B3n.jpg

14 User: Rémih uploaded the original photograph (a faithful reproduction of public domain hieroglyphs); User:-sche removed the yellow-green tint. CC BY-SA 3.0 <http://creativecommons.org/licenses/by-sa/3.0/>, via Wikimedia Commons: https://commons.wikimedia.org/wiki/File:Edfu_15_cartouche_hieroglyphs_decolorized.jpg

15 Pearson Scott Foresman, Public domain, via Wikimedia Commons: https://commons.wikimedia.org/wiki/File:Uraeus_(PSF).png

16 George Douros, Public domain, via Wikimedia Commons: https://commons.wikimedia.org/wiki/File:Abydos-Bold-hieroglyph-N35A.png

17 US Government (Central Intelligence Agency), Public domain, via Wikimedia Commons: https://commons.wikimedia.org/wiki/File:Physical_Map_of_Africa_(2021).svg

18 Bukulu Steven, CC BY-SA 4.0 <https://creativecommons.org/licenses/by-sa/4.0>, via Wikimedia Commons: https://commons.wikimedia.org/wiki/File:African_neckless_2.JPG

19 Ji-Elle, CC BY-SA 3.0 <https://creativecommons.org/licenses/by-sa/3.0>, via Wikimedia Commons: https://commons.wikimedia.org/wiki/File:Pot_et_collier_Luba-Mus%C3%A9e_royal_de_l%27Afrique_centrale.jpg

20 Cezary p at pl.Wikipedia, CC BY-SA 3.0 <http://creativecommons.org/licenses/by-sa/3.0/>, via Wikimedia Commons: https://commons.wikimedia.org/wiki/File:African_wooden_mask.jpg

21 Brooklyn Museum, CC BY 3.0 <https://creativecommons.org/licenses/by/3.0>, via Wikimedia Commons: https://commons.wikimedia.org/wiki/File:Brooklyn_Museum_22.1411_Spear_(2).jpg

22 Szaaman, Public domain, via Wikimedia Commons: https://commons.wikimedia.org/wiki/File:Gold_bullion_1.jpg

23 Ragesoss, CC BY-SA 3.0 <https://creativecommons.org/licenses/by-sa/3.0>, via Wikimedia Commons: https://commons.wikimedia.org/wiki/File:Raffia_fibers.jpg

24 Bukky658, CC BY-SA 4.0 <https://creativecommons.org/licenses/by-sa/4.0>, via Wikimedia Commons: https://commons.wikimedia.org/wiki/File:Local_grinding_stone.jpg

25 Ji-Elle, CC BY-SA 4.0 <https://creativecommons.org/licenses/by-sa/4.0>, via Wikimedia Commons: https://commons.wikimedia.org/wiki/File:Statue_mpwuu_Yanzi-Mus%C3%A9e_royal_de_l%27Afrique_centrale.jpg

26 one_click_beyond, CC BY 2.5 <https://creativecommons.org/licenses/by/2.5>, via Wikimedia Commons: https://commons.wikimedia.org/wiki/File:WLA_brooklynmuseum_20th_century_hoe.jpg

27 Tsinkala, CC BY-SA 4.0 <https://creativecommons.org/licenses/by-sa/4.0>, via Wikimedia Commons: https://commons.wikimedia.org/wiki/File:African_Traditional_Drum_on_Sale.jpg

Printed in Dunstable, United Kingdom